What Others Are Saying about This Book . . .

Simply a beautiful book about life, love, and purpose.
—Jack Canfield, coauthor, *Chicken Soup for the Soul*

A touching portrait of a remarkable dog. If you're looking for a feel-good story, this is it.
—Jamie Hall, *Edmonton Journal*

In a perfect world, every dog would have a home and every home would have a dog—like Toby!
—Nina Siemaszko, actress, *The West Wing*

A captivating, heartwarming story.
—Steve Hudis, producer, IMPACT Motion Pictures

Toby has been one of my all-time favorite interviews; he is right next to Bob Barker and Gordie Howe! His capacity to spread cheer is truly inspirational!
—Mindy Tweedle, producer/host, CTS TV

This is a meaningful and moving story in which we can all find truth.
—Justin Hines, award-winning singer/songwriter

A heart
living w   636.7
          Hammc
          On Tc

y about

‹ *Times*
ffortless
Purpose

As with people, and as this book shows, providing your dog with a purpose will give you a happy and satisfied pet.

—Karin Overgaard, Certified Pet
Dog Trainer (CPDT-KA),
Certified Master Trainer (CMT)

They say when the student is ready, the teacher appears. This is an amazing story that will wake up the student in you.

—Aubrey Winfield, president, Orange
Media Group of Companies

Enjoy the relationship learning adventure of both pet and human in this delightful book.

—Kaytie Stack, K9 Awareness

Dogs are affected by the energy from our emotions and thoughts. This insight was both luck, and labor, for Toby.

—Robin McKay, Jin Shin Jyutsu practitioner

Living with an open mind and heart is but one of the insightful lessons taught by this incredible animal in this lovely book.

—Lisa Litwinski, LIT PATH Learning Centre Ltd.

Authentically moving!

—Shawne Duperon, Producer,
Six-time Emmy award winner

On TOBY's Terms

CHARMAINE HAMMOND

BYB
BETTIE YOUNGS BOOKS

Cover design by Tatomir A. Pitariu and Jane Hagaman
Cover photo by Christopher J. Alcock

If you are unable to order this book from your local bookseller,
you may order directly from the publisher.

BETTIE YOUNGS BOOK PUBLISHERS
www.BettieYoungsBooks.com

BETTIE YOUNGS BOOKS are distributed by
SCB Distributors
www.SCBdistributors.com
800/729-6423

Library of Congress Control Number: 2010930780

ISBN: 978-0-9843081-4-9
10 9 8 7 6 5 4 3 2
Printed in the USA

To Toby . . . for teaching me
that your terms matter, too.

Contents

Foreword

For the past thirty years, I have been training and working my dogs, as well as helping other people to understand their own canine companions. I've titled dogs in obedience and tracking, ran joyously with them through agility courses, battled the elements together in search and rescue, and experienced the communication and ultimate bond of trust needed to work a dog in explosive detection.

The result of all that experience, combined with an instinctual ability to "read" a dog (interpret its body language and signals), has provided me with a deeper insight into understanding and improving the interactions between dogs and their humans. When it came to human/canine relationships, I thought I had seen it all.

Until I met Toby.

Charmaine Hammond contacted me because she and her husband Christopher were having some "issues" with a Chesapeake Bay retriever they had recently adopted. Charmaine described Toby as a wonderful dog—loving, kind, extremely intelligent—but with a "few quirks and an assortment of odd habits." These included . . . well, let's just say that the Hammonds had to buy toilet tank lids by the case, and that's just the beginning.

All dogs, not just Toby, are complex animals. They have an amazing ability to read and interpret body language, both within their canine community and their human family; have the capacity to detect changes in our body chemistry that may pinpoint diseases, as well as mood changes or emotional upheaval in their owners; and they have a compelling desire to know where they fit into your family dynamic in order to coexist peacefully.

By observing and learning to read the signals your dog exhibits, you can better appreciate your dog's sensitivity and loyalty to you, as well as anticipate and divert unwanted behaviors. If you provide a clear order and consistency to its life, your dog can relax into its role within your family structure. Some dogs can be "social climbers" and will try to work their way up the pecking order if the rules aren't established. A working partnership with a dog is based on mutual trust. Once you learn to trust in your canine's intentions and capabilities, you can both approach your relationship using your instincts—which come from the heart, not the mind. All these things and more we worked on to help Toby better fit into his new family.

Still, I have heard some strange stories in my career, and Toby wins "paws down" for originality, including the positive effect he has had on innumerable lives. In the end, Toby outsmarted us all. I highly recommend this book to anyone who has ever loved a dog, wanted a dog . . . or wondered what to do with the dog they've got.

Maggie Schlegl, Behaviorist
Capable Canines

A Word from the Author

I have had many "wake up calls" in life, several of which you will read about in this book. Then along came Toby, the five-year-old Chesapeake Bay retriever my husband and I decided to bring into our lives. Toby was one of those wake up calls . . .

I believe that every challenge is accompanied by a gift, and I was about to discover that many gifts are accompanied by a challenge!

My husband and I never imagined how this dog would change our lives. They say the teacher appears when the student is ready; what we were about to learn is that perhaps we were the students . . . and not the teachers.

This is the story of Toby.

Enjoy it, and be blessed.

Acknowledgments

First, all my love and many thanks to my husband, Christopher Alcock. Thank you for your unwavering devotion to me and for your comments on this story—and for not giving up on Toby. Growing with you has been a precious experience and one for which I am honored and grateful. To mom and dad, Josie and Ken Hammond, always you helped me to believe in myself—thank for that gift. Your love, support, and encouragement throughout my life has been succor to my heart and soul! To Adele and Melanie for your sisterly love and for the great memories growing up! To my amazing niece, Ashley, for being a source of joy in our lives. To my best friend of some forty years, Rose Anne, for the many ways you provided support during the writing of this book; I treasure our friendship!

Bettie Youngs, our publisher and friend, helped me discover the story that needed to be told. Thank you for your guidance and mentoring in what has turned into a most amazing journey. A huge thank you to Faith Farthing, Tricia Radison, and Laura Cappello Bromling of FinalEyes Communications, Inc., and to Tania Seymour for your editorial expertise. Thank you to Randee Feldman of GET NOTICED Public Relations for your creativity in helping us share the word and the fun we had along the way!

Two PAWS up for the staff and volunteers with Chimo Animal Assisted Therapy Project and to the Northern Alberta Society for Animal Protection for the very important work you do and, most especially, for being there for Toby.

Special thanks to Maggie, animal behaviorist and friend, for helping us help Toby. To Sarah, Terry, Drell, Sharon, and the staff and patients at the hospital where Toby volunteers: you have made a difference in Toby's life and ours, and I thank you for that. A big "woof!" to all Toby's four-legged and two-legged friends who make our lives interesting, especially Toby's BFF, Lauren.

A special thanks to Guiliana Temme for sharing her wonderful story! Thanks to Jane Hagaman for the "pawsitively" fun interior design on this book!

And lastly, to our extraordinary dog Toby for the joy, love, laughs, and special moments you have added to our lives! We will treasure them always.

One

Oh, Toby!

You never know when your life is going to change.

"Hi, honey," I said into my cell phone as I unlocked my car. "I gave my presentation; it went great, and I'm on my way home. How was your day?"

"My day was wonderful . . . until I walked into the house."

"Uh-oh . . ."

"The place is a total disaster. *Your* dog knocked over all four dining room chairs, the lamp in the living room, and that little table your mom gave you."

"My dog?" I sank into the driver's seat, clutching my cell phone, suddenly dreading the three-hour drive from Calgary back to Edmonton because of what I envisioned I'd find when I got home.

"I'm at my wits' end, Char. There's mud and blood everywhere."

I froze in the act of turning the ignition key. "Blood?"

"That darned dog climbed on the kitchen counter, knocked over the knife block, and cut two of his feet. Then he tracked blood all over the kitchen, the living room, the hallways, the basement . . ."

"Is he okay?"

"Is *he* okay? What about *me?*"

I cringed at the volume of his voice. "I'm sorry, honey," I said, visualizing our eighty-five pound Chesapeake Bay retriever walking across the kitchen counter, the sink, and stove, tracking blood. "How bad are his cuts?"

"Not too bad, but I had to pin him down to get his feet cleaned up and bandage his two front paws. He'll live." Christopher didn't sound altogether pleased at the prospect.

Under other circumstances, a vision of my normally mild-mannered and easygoing husband chasing our dog through the house might have been amusing. But not now. Apart from the cut feet, which was a new twist, this was not the first—or the second, or the third—disaster we'd faced since bringing Toby into our home a few months earlier. It was peculiar, because for the first few weeks after we got him, things had been quite uneventful. But now one incident led to another.

"There's more," Chris said. "He knocked the books and candles off the coffee table and tipped the wooden table in the foyer over so it was blocking the door. I could barely get in. The flower planters were knocked over and so was the water cooler, which had a full canister of water in it this morning. Not now. Now the water's all over our nice hard-wood floor. That damn dog tore the boot racks from the closet wall and emptied the contents into the front entrance. He tracked bloody footprints all over the down-stairs carpet. The house looks like a crime scene."

"It can't be that bad."

"It can't? You wouldn't recognize the kitchen or living room. Char, when I assess all the damage caused by this unruly, incorrigible, untrained, ill-mannered, and soon-to-have-another-home dog . . ."

"Don't say that. I know there have been some problems, but Toby's a great dog in so many ways. He's just got a lit-tle problem and we'll fix it."

"A *little* problem? You should see the phone in the kitchen. It's bloody, too. Maybe he was trying to call 9-1-1."

"That's funny, Chris!" I laughed. "Just hang on, honey. I'll be home soon."

"*Not* funny," my dear husband replied. "I've had it this time. I'm done with that dog!"

"Please, just hang on. When I get home, I'll help you clean up after my . . . after *our* dog."

I heard him release a deep breath. "We can't keep living on Toby's terms."

But lately we were.

911?

TWO

Adopting and Adapting

Things hadn't always been this way, of course. Originally, Toby had seemed to be the fulfillment of Chris's and my dreams. I thought about that as I drove north from Calgary back toward Edmonton. How could things have gone so bad so fast?

Ironically, it had been Chris who first showed Toby to me, or rather called me to the computer to look at Toby's big, grinning mug on a website dedicated to rescue animals. At that point, a year had passed since the death of our previous dog, Dooks. Chris and I had gotten past the grief and were feeling the hollow place in our lives where our beloved German shepherd had lived. We were ready for another dog, but because we both worked jobs that took us away from home, we wanted a mature animal, not a puppy. The last thing we needed was chewed furniture and messes on the carpet.

"Look, it's a Chesapeake Bay retriever," Chris said, "just like the one we saw at the SPCA. His name is Toby, he's five years old, and he's in a rescue agency in Sherwood Park, so he's a local."

I looked at the picture of a big, dark-brown dog with floppy ears and a white spot on his chest and felt drawn to him instantly. Who could resist a dog who smiled for the camera?

According to the website, Toby had been in foster care for the last three months, and for some reason I felt a strong sense of urgency about him. "Let's call," I said. "Right now. Let's do it."

We left a message with the local rescue agency, and I filled out the online application form.

Then we waited.

Days passed.

Nothing.

"Perhaps something was wrong with the computer system or the application," Christopher said. "Maybe we should call."

As I picked up the phone, he asked me what I'd written on the application form.

"I just answered the questions."

"Did you tell them that because of all we can offer a dog, why we'd be great parents?"

"Well, I hope so. I zeroed in on supplying the information they requested, like this one, which asks about what our plans are to take care of a dog. I put that we have time to exercise it, take it to the off-leash park so it can run free and play with other dogs, and participate in obedience classes."

Christopher's face said everything.

"Should I redo the application?"

"Yes. They need to know we're really ready to love and care for this dog. They want to know how much we really *want* a dog."

He was absolutely right. I wondered about the lack of detail I had used on the application. Why had I put so little effort into it? Surely they were looking for our willingness to love and care for this dog. And they'd find the answer in the emotional tone of our value-laden response. In one of my previous careers, I had facilitated open human adoptions, helping birth mothers select the family who would adopt her child. I had seen firsthand the care taken by prospective adoptive parents to make sure both the birth mother and I understood the qualities and values that were important to them.

So I needed to bring that quality of thoughtfulness to this application for our adopting Toby. I didn't know if the folks surrendering him would be reading my application, but this time I decided to complete it as if they would be, because surely they, like the birth mothers I had worked with, would want their beloved "child" to be adopted by the best and most loving family.

As I filled out the application again, I recalled one of the most precious experiences I'd once had while working as a counselor and mediator, in which I'd held a private contract with an adoption agency. One of clients, a young woman, had gone into labor, and her birthing coach could not make it to the hospital. So I went. When I arrived, the woman asked me to be by her side during the birth of her baby.

Never having had a child myself, I didn't know what to expect, but I did know giving birth was a sacred event; the woman was so young, and I felt for her. I reassured her that I'd be right there for her: It had given her great comfort.

During her labor, I held her hand and just supported her as best I could. Within hours, a beautiful and healthy baby was born to this young woman, and then she had to face the most difficult decision ever—giving her new infant, her son, up for adoption.

To this day, I have no words to describe the emotions I felt during that life-altering experience. So many mixed emotions. On the one hand, I was overjoyed that the baby was healthy and that his mother had come through the delivery so well; on the other, I was deeply saddened that she would soon be saying goodbye to her child . . . yet also happy for the family who would finally have a child to love.

For the parents to be, that a baby had come into their lives was a dream come true. Their yearning for a child finally fulfilled.

I was there when she met the adoptive family and saw the connection between them even before the first word was exchanged. I could see that she knew that these were the right people for her child, that they could cherish and care for him in a way that she was unable to do. Gratitude poured from both the family and the mother, forming a bond that I don't think anyone who hadn't gone through this experience could understand.

I watched as the young mother handed over her baby

and, with tears in her eyes, gave him to the new parents. My knees weak, I left the hospital; once I got to my car, I just cried and cried. I cried for everyone's joy . . . and pain. I will never forget what it must have been like for this young woman to make the selfless decision, out of love for her baby, to give him up.

As I continued my drive, thinking back on all this, it seemed incredible how much effort we had put into getting Toby. When I once again responded to the questions on the application, the words flowed from my heart not my head.

One section asked about where the dog would stay, the setup of the house, and if there was a yard. I wrote that we had a dog door leading from the kitchen into the backyard, which would allow Toby to go outside when we were away from the house. I described the beautiful park our home backed onto and our cottage on the lake where we spent weekends and most of the summer months. Our lifestyle would provide Toby with a great deal of exercise, variety, and excitement. Although I gave motivational workshops to businesses around Canada, and Chris worked as a manager and land surveyor for a local geomatics firm, I worked out of my home office between trips, and Chris's office was located nearby. We might not always be home, but Toby's time alone would be limited.

Another question inquired about our experience with animals. Well, that was an easy one. Although Chris's family had not owned a pet until Chris was in high school, I had grown up around animals. Duchess, my family's first dog—kind, gentle, and well behaved, living up to her regal name. Frisky, a little black dog full of energy, whose name said it all. Several cats. A budgie bird. A rabbit. A gerbil. There had once even been twenty newly hatched chicks in the house, from when I was given the honor of bringing my kindergarten class's clutch of eggs home over Easter vacation.

I'd loved them all. Including the tank of guppies—even though they met their demise on the day my younger sister Adele decided to do a good deed and clean my fish for me. Sporting her little yellow crocheted dusting hat, she netted each fish from the tank and lay them in a towel, then she sprayed them with glass cleaner and gave them a good scrub. Once all the fish were dry, she put them back in the aquarium. They didn't ever swim again, though they did float quite nicely.

Then I got my very own cat, Spooky, when, after getting an apartment following college, I needed a house companion.

So when I answered the question: "In what way are you prepared to deal with the trials and tribulations of owning a pet?"—I had no problem explaining how experienced I was in that department!

Application finished, I read Christopher the answers, and he added some information of his own. "Our ball-throwing arms are in great shape," and "We think Toby is just waiting to come into our lives . . . we can just feel it."

Christopher and I carefully read each and every question again and again, and finally pleased, pressed "Send"— this time more confident we'd shown the agency that we would be a good match for this dog.

"The rescue agent would be negligent if they denied

Toby the opportunity to have us in his life," Christopher remarked.

The very next day, the rescue agency called to tell us they'd received our application, and would like to meet us . . . and have us meet Toby at the home of his foster-care "parents."

Three

Prozac Dog

After an hour and a half on the road, I pulled into a gas station. While the tank filled, I went inside the store and picked up a coffee and a mild pepperoni stick, a treat Toby loved but rarely got. As I carried it to the counter I thought about how Chris would view the treat—rightfully—as a reward for bad behavior. He wouldn't approve. *I've had it this time. I'm done with that dog, Char.* But I couldn't help it. Despite everything, I missed Toby, and I knew he couldn't be having a good time at home with my not-very-happy husband.

As I stood at the counter in the gas station, waiting to pay for my coffee and pepperoni stick, the cashier rang the order up with one hand while holding the phone to her ear with the other. "Listen, missy," she barked into the receiver,

"I don't want to hear your excuses. I want that kitchen clean when I get home. If you do a good job, I'll bring you that candy bar. If not, you get nothing." She hung up and shook her head.

"Kids?" I said.

"Yeah. Just trying to put the fear of God into my fourteen-year-old so she won't leave the kitchen in the usual mess. But so far, I'm batting zero. That's a dollar for the pepperoni." As I handed her the money, she added, "Is that for you or bribing the kids?"

"The kid," I replied, and we laughed.

As I got back on the road, I reflected on the day we first met Toby.

Toby's foster caretakers, Yasmin and David, not only cared for rescue dogs but bred Rhodesian ridgebacks. Over the years, they had fostered more than forty dogs, and their love of and skill with canines was evident in everything they said. After chatting for several minutes at the kitchen table, we seemed to have passed the first litmus test of approval, too.

They called for Toby.

With a wild thumping and clattering, three dogs came bounding across the kitchen floor, all curious to check us out. The biggest dog was Toby himself, a sturdy animal with a chocolate-brown coat tinged with auburn, his tongue and lips standing out against it in vibrant pink, his eyes an arresting combination of yellow and brown. His hair grew wavy around his dog collar, making his head and neck look much larger than they turned out to really be.

He nudged my leg, sniffed my feet, licked my hand.

After giving Chris a quick sniff, he went over to visit David.

During this sensory evaluation, we humans continued talking, and I noticed that every time Toby's name was mentioned he'd look at the speaker and then at the others in the conversation, moving his head to follow whoever spoke next.

Jack, a little Jack Russell terrier, was most curious about us newcomers, and when he came to check us out, Toby left David's side and returned to us as well. His nose was wet, his eyes bright, his tail wagging like a propeller about to make him take flight. But it was his face that most captivated me—remarkably expressive and energetic, it made me think of a child bursting with excitement.

I told Chris, "His ears feel like velvet."

The more I petted Toby, the happier he seemed. Still, when Jack nudged my leg to get in on the cuddling action, Toby moved amiably aside. For a big dog, he appeared to be very gentle—another appealing quality.

After a moment I felt a big paw on my knee and looked up to find Toby staring at me again. "What do you want, Toby?" I asked. "Do you want to play?"

At the sound of the "P" word, his ears perked up, his tail began rotoring, and he backed up to give me enough room to stand. His every movement cried, *Come play! Come play!*

What an interesting dog, I thought. Looking into his eyes again, I felt myself falling in love. His gaze was different from our previous dog, Dooks's, had been—or, for that matter, the gaze of any other dog I had ever known; it left me feeling like I had just been hugged. I glanced at my husband, who smiled; he had sensed it, too.

My heart told me I already loved this animal. I was sold.

David and Yasmin gave us a little bit of Toby's story. He had weighed 125 pounds when his original owner surrendered him, making him more than thirty-five pounds overweight for a dog of his breed and age—five years old at the time. He had obviously not been well exercised, and Yasmin admitted he had had health issues and had to take several medications.

"That's hard to believe. He looks pretty healthy," said Chris, carefully eyeing Toby.

"When Toby came to us, he needed help with separation anxiety and other problems," Yasmin remarked. "He had a big bag of medications for ear infections and eye problems, plus Prozac and a canine antidepressant."

"A *what?*" Chris asked.

Yasmin nodded. "He was really depressed when we got him."

I asked what his previous owners had been like.

"The good news is that we have no reason to be concerned about abuse or neglect. Toby's owners were an elderly couple. They loved him, perhaps too much—they overfed him as a way of showing their love. When the man passed away, Toby was very affected. In fact, we understand it was Toby who alerted the wife that something was wrong with her husband."

"That's amazing," I said, scratching Toby's ears.

"Unfortunately, he was just too much of a handful for the wife by herself, so she surrendered him. But it's clear this was an animal who was loved."

As Yasmin talked, I looked into Toby's eyes and felt sadness wash over me. I could only imagine how hard it must have been for his owner to give away her dog at the same time she was grieving the loss of a spouse.

With my mind occupied by this thought, the phrase "just too much of a handful" sailed right past me.

Yasmin continued: "We were shocked at just how overweight Toby was and how damaged his coat was. So the first thing we did after meeting with the vet was to take him off the medications, change his food and eating routines, and get him back to health. His eyelids improved, the infections went away, and as you can see, his coat is healthy."

"That's incredible progress in three months," I said.

"We got him exercising regularly, too," Yasmin said. "Dave always runs the dogs when he gets home from work, and it didn't take long before Toby was keeping up with the pack. Then, because Toby is a retriever and a water dog, Dave decided to take him to a park with a small lake and toss a ball into the water. Toby raced right in after it . . . but after a few seconds Dave thought he was going to have to jump in and save him. Turns out Toby didn't really know how to swim."

We all laughed. Even Toby seemed to grin. "How is he with your other dogs?" I asked. "There are a lot of dogs on the cul-de-sac where we live."

"Initially, he was a little protective of his toys, but he shares them now. And he taught our pup Keesha to fetch, which is surprising because ridgebacks enjoy chasing a ball but don't typically bring it back. They aren't retrievers. We're not sure how he managed to teach her to go against her nature, but my sense is that it's because Toby is extremely social, and he just persisted with Keesha until she learned what he wanted her to learn. He's a very smart dog."

"I can see that." Watching Toby, I found it hard to believe he had once been overweight, sluggish, and unhappy. He seemed so animated, so full of joy. I glanced at Christopher to see if he was as taken with this dog as I was.

At that same moment, Toby left me, went to Chris and nudged his hand, as if suddenly more interested in my husband's approval than mine. Christopher smiled. "He's a nice dog."

"Right," David said in his clipped British accent. "Come on, let's see how he reacts to the both of you. Toby, let's go outside."

Toby scrambled away, tail swinging wildly.

"Aha," I said. "Looks like he knows English."

"Oh, yes," said David in a serious voice. "In fact, I suspect Toby knows a lot more than we think he does."

Four

Settling In

"Toby, fetch!" In Yasmin and David's backyard, Christopher tossed a toy for Toby to chase. Toby raced off with Jack the Jack Russell terrier and a small herd of ridgebacks following closely. Sprinting across the lawn, Toby grabbed the toy, swung around, and bounded back. Proudly, he dropped the toy and barked a rather thunderous bark: *Again! Again!* Christopher complied and off the pack went—Toby, Jack, and seven ridgebacks, enjoying their game on a sunny Saturday afternoon. Again, Toby dropped the toy at Christopher's feet and barked. *Hurry! Again!*

Twenty minutes later, Chris came to the conclusion that this dog would play fetch until time ended or Chris's arm gave out, whichever came first. But by then we had had plenty of opportunity to see that Toby was comfortable around other dogs and showed no signs of aggression or territorial behavior.

"Well," Chris said, rubbing his arm, "he'll definitely give us *our* exercise."

"Look at him with all these dogs," I said. "If he's like this at the dog park, we'll have no problem letting him off his leash."

Toby chose that moment to take a break from playing and plunk himself beside me. Nuzzling his head into my thigh, he gazed up at me. *Pet me, lady.* "Chris," I said, "he is adorable." I was ready to take him home on the spot.

Christopher nodded thoughtfully. He seemed to like Toby, but true to his nature, he was reluctant to make a decision based on emotion. Practicalities were important, too. Besides, the adoption process required us to "sleep on it" before deciding.

Chris turned to David. "So he's basically healthy now?"

"Very healthy. He's at a good weight, and if you continue to exercise him, he'll lose even more."

"Good with kids? We don't have any, but I don't want a dog that might bite someone else's kid."

"Not a problem. We take Toby to the off-leash park, and he's nothing but gentle around the children there."

"That's great," I said. "We have a lot of young children in our neighborhood."

David smiled. "Then Toby will be in his glory. He's very social, playful, and reliable around people. I think he'll make someone a great playmate."

"Yasmin mentioned separation anxiety," I said. "What's he like when he's left alone?"

David shrugged. "At first he would get anxious when we

were away from him, even if we were just in another room. Pacing, barking. But now he settles right down. He knows we're coming back—and you've seen the action around here. There's always somebody around, human or dog, so he's never really alone, but I don't see him having a problem once he settles in with you."

"You two are just what Toby needs," said Yasmin, as she walked us back out to our truck. "I can tell when a dog and a person are right for each other, and I really think Toby will excel with you two."

Christopher said nothing. As we pulled away, I asked him what he thought.

"Let's see how we feel in the morning."

"Really?" I was amazed. Personally, I was so certain about Toby . . .

Chris smiled and squeezed my hand. "Not really. He's great. Let's make him ours."

The next day, Chris and I returned to David and Yasmin's place to pick up the new member of our family. The moment we got home and Christopher opened the door into the house, Toby squeezed past him and began roaming from room to room, sniffing furniture, poking his nose into the coat closet, giving everything a good once-over. He was curious but also somewhat tentative; when his tail brushed our palm plant, he jumped back with a loud bark.

Christopher opened the patio door off the kitchen, and Toby raced out to the backyard, where he proceeded to give each bush and tree a sniff and then mark his territory. I wondered if he could still smell evidence of Dooks' reign in our home.

When Christopher retired to the living room to watch television, I busied myself with housecleaning and opening the mail. At the same time, I kept one eye on Toby. I wanted him to know I was close by, while giving him the freedom to familiarize himself with his new surroundings.

For a while, Toby kept up his restless roaming and sniffing, but as the day wore on, he grew quiet and then almost shy. He curled up on the rug in the living room and just lay there, following me with his eyes but refusing to come when I called him.

Thinking he needed reassurance, I squatted down and said, "You're home to stay now, Toby."

His tail swished, but his gaze lacked the brightness I had seen at the foster family's home. For once I couldn't read his thoughts.

I put my arms around his neck. "Do you miss your other home? I know you must be sad without all your four-legged friends. It is going to be a lot more quiet here. . . ."

His gaze finally grew more intense, filled with that focused concentration. Still, he did not look particularly happy, so I took him outside to play fetch since I knew fetch was his favorite game.

As I threw the toy, I kept talking to him in a bright and cheery tone. "You're going to love living here, Toby. Chris and I are a lot of fun . . .

"We have a cottage on the lake where you can swim in the summer . . . oh, that's right, we might have to teach you how to swim . . .

"We have a dog door here in the kitchen, so you can go into the backyard whenever you need to . . .

"Chris told me he's more than willing to help you learn how to fetch his paper . . .

"There are kids next door and plenty of others in the cul-de-sac, so you'll have lots of little friends to play with . . .

"Yup. You lucked out, buddy-boy . . ."

Although Toby dutifully ran after the toy and returned to drop it at my feet, his demeanor seemed uncertain and anxious—as if he were only going through the motions of playing catch. *I'll do this because it seems to be important to you, but really, what's the point?*

But I didn't worry about it. Of course he was out of sorts. Of course he was nervous. This was another big change for him; he'd need time to adjust to his new surroundings.

He'd be fine.

Five

And So It Begins . . .

See, I thought to myself as I drove, *everything started out great. So what happened?*

At first, my assessment of Toby's situation seemed to be correct. In time, he did start to settle in to his new circumstances; in fact, he thrived. We trained him to go through the dog door, and were surprised at how fast he caught on to the technique. We were even more pleased with how well-behaved he was on walks. On the leash, he walked calmly right beside us, even with the distractions of passing children or other dogs. Even better, if we released him from the leash he would come back promptly when called—unlike Dooks, who was apt to disappear on us.

Of course, that might not have been much of a training

accomplishment. The truth was that even when Toby was off-leash, he didn't seem to want to be more than a few feet ahead of us. This was a dog who yearned to be close to his owners all the time.

Really close.

Constantly close.

In fact, we began to notice that Toby was always underfoot. If Chris or I got up from the couch, Toby was right there on our heels. If we turned around, Toby turned around. Chris collided with Toby each time he pivoted while pacing and talking on the phone. If I wanted to use the shower, I had to either sprint for the bathroom when Toby wasn't looking, or expect to shower with a retriever gazing at me through the glass door.

"I think I'm going to rename him Shadow," said Christopher one evening after tripping over Toby for the third time—and tripping over a Chesapeake Bay retriever is not a minor experience.

As time went on, we noticed that Toby had some other rather odd habits. In fact, in his own way, he seemed to be a creature of exotic habits. For example, at dinnertime, he would always bolt for the bathroom. We had no idea why. And every time I blew-dry my hair, Toby would materialize, sitting almost on my feet. "This is weird, Christopher," I said. "The second I pick up the blow-dryer, he's right at my side. It's like he knows when I'm going to dry my hair. Do you think he's protecting me from the blow-dryer?"

"Or maybe he realizes that you're often about to go out when you dry your hair," Chris suggested.

"That's a good theory. I just hope it's not the separation anxiety Yasmin mentioned."

Perhaps I shouldn't have expressed my fears aloud. We soon came to recognize the signs of just how anxious Toby became when he suspected he was going to be left alone. As Chris or I prepared to leave, Toby would begin to fuss around, pacing, following us to the door—and on some occasions, walking right into the garage as if to join whoever was departing.

This being alone thing seemed to be a real issue for Toby, so, to get him used to solitude in his new home, we practiced leaving and then returning after a very short absence, so he would understand that we always did return.

It didn't work. The anxious predeparture pacing continued.

We also noticed that no matter how long we were gone, when we came home Toby always met us right at the door. I found myself wondering if he had even moved from that spot the entire time we were away.

Still, it was nothing to worry about; this behavior fell into the category of "harmless quirk." We got used to it.

Then came The Day. Chris and I had to go out to run a few short errands. We wouldn't be gone long and decided to leave Toby behind. He did his pacing thing as we headed for the door . . . nothing unusual.

But when we got back home, something had changed. We couldn't open the door between the garage and the house. It was blocked.

"What the heck?" I said. I could hear the eager clacking sound of Toby's claws inside, signaling *They're home! They're home!* But the door wouldn't budge, and we finally had to go around back and let ourselves in through the rear door.

As we stepped inside the house, Toby danced around us in a strange, mixed choreography of joy and cringing. I patted his head as we walked toward the front of the house—then halted with a jolt. What appeared to be the entire contents of our front hall closet—shoes, hats, gloves, umbrellas, even the shoe rack—had been dragged down the middle of the foyer and piled in front of the door to the garage.

I looked at Toby, who skittered around us: *You're home! I'm sorry about this mess . . . You're home! I'm sorry about this mess . . . You're home!*

Chris and I stared at one another in astonishment, then surveyed the damage more closely. Inside the closet, most of the hangers hung empty—the coats were part of the big pile in the hallway. In fact, almost the only items that belonged in the closet and were still in there were on the top shelf, out of Toby's reach.

Then I noticed that the closet wasn't the only victim of Toby's inexplicable frenzy. A small table that my parents had restored —actually an old schoolhouse desk with an inkwell hole—had been shifted into the middle of the foyer. The items that had been inside it—keys, poop-bags, and Toby's leash—were now on the floor. Toby's nice soft bed lay atop the shoes. The rug that was supposed to lie in front of the door had made its way to the far side of the foyer.

The good news was that none of the items had been damaged or chewed, just . . . rearranged.

I had no idea what could have brought on this behavior and neither did Chris—but because it was the first time anything like this had happened, we simply told Toby, "Bad boy!" and put all our possessions back where they belonged.

We were sure it would never happen again.

We were wrong.

Soon we knew for a fact that Toby didn't always spend the time while we were away sitting expectantly in front of the door. Sometimes—not always, but often enough to makes us dread approaching our home—Toby spent his alone time finding increasingly creative ways to trash our house.

On top of that, he began to exhibit more and more odd quirks, a whole catalogue of aberrant behaviors, even when we *were* at home.

One of the worst was his habit of disrupting dinnertime. At some point between the setting of the table and the cleaning up afterward, Toby would walk over to his dog door, poke his nose outside, bark two or three times, then turn and head into the main-floor bathroom. Next, as predictably as sunrise, a loud *rattle-rattle-rattle* would echo through the house as he banged the shower door with his nose: exactly three times, enough to knock the shampoo bottle into the tub. During this ritual, Toby's rump would nudge the bathroom door shut behind him, trapping him in the room. If he wasn't rescued immediately, he would start banging the toilet seat up and down with his nose until someone came to release him.

The first couple of times this happened it was kind of funny, a colorful extension of his earlier habit of shutting himself into random rooms when Christopher and I were gone. But soon it became infuriating. For more than a decade, Chris and I had been able to eat dinner in peace. After a long day of work, the last thing either of us wanted was to have our tranquil meal interrupted by this racket. Nor did either of us much want to jump up from the table and deal with a dog who had somehow managed to make our time together all about him.

Then there was the bowl-spinning—another obvious attempt to capture our undying attention. At odd times of the day or night, Toby would get his metal food dish rotating in its frame, creating the sound of a plane taking off. The roar was so loud it would either disturb us in our offices or wake us from sleep, and Toby would keep at it until one of us charged into the kitchen and snapped: "Toby! Stop it right now!" Then, goal attained, he'd stare at the wall—the picture of innocence.

Toby was not so innocent when he was caught following people into the washroom. His fascination with washrooms stumped us. Anyone, including a visitor, might walk into our washroom and turn around to shut the door, only to find a smiling Toby standing there, too. When ushered out, Toby always seemed surprised, as if he couldn't fathom why he was being asked to leave.

In addition to his fetishes, Toby had his fears. One day, I set about baking a banana cake, a rare treat. The moment I turned on the mixer, Toby leaped off his bed and bolted over to me.

"What's up, Toby? You don't like this noise? It's okay. . . ." My soothing words didn't help. Toby forced himself between me and the cupboard and sat there the entire time I mixed the batter.

When Chris got home, he kissed my cheek and said, "Mmmm, it smells good in here. What did you bake for me?"

"Banana cake, my mom's recipe this time."

"Excellent." He walked over to the pile of mail on the counter. "So how was Toby today?"

"Good, except he kind of freaked out when I ran the mixer. He did the same thing a couple of days ago with the coffee grinder and my color printer. When the printer turned on, he left the room entirely."

Chris flipped through some envelopes. "Strange . . . come to think of it, he got pretty antsy that time I used the air compressor to pump up the tires on the Blazer, too."

A few days later I learned about another loud noise Toby didn't care for. I had just sat down to tackle some emails and phone messages when Toby began pacing around the house, the clicking his nails on the hardwood floor was quite distracting. "Toby, come," I said, patting his mat for him to lie down. He did so, but two seconds later, he was up and pacing again. "Toby, what's going on?"

That was when I heard the grinding roar of the garbage truck pulling onto our street, followed by loud barking as Toby frantically raced from room to room, apparently trying to get away from the noise of the garbage canisters being emptied into the truck. The recycling truck followed shortly behind, creating even more noise and getting even more of a reaction.

I added "garbage truck" to the mental list of the noises that disturbed Toby.

But it was the escalating level of destructiveness that really bothered Chris and me.

"I don't know what gets into him, Char," said Chris. "I slipped out the door to chat with our neighbor, and I didn't even think to close the bathroom door. I was only gone for fifteen minutes . . ."

"Oh, no, what happened?"

"The usual. Everything that had been on the counter

was on the floor. The toilet tank lid was smashed and both taps were running water full blast. How does he turn on the water? And how many toilet tank lids are we going to have to go through?"

"I think we're up to nine, right?" I was joking—it had only been five. Still, how many people have to replace their toilet tank lid even once?

Whatever Toby was reacting to—loud noises, inattention, or the boredom of being left alone—he was beginning to cause serious and expensive damage to our home and our emotions. The "Toby disaster fund" was beginning to run dry.

Especially with my husband.

Six

He's Gone

With all these memories floating around in my head, I finally reached home. I opened the front door slowly, nervous about the state of the house—and the state of my husband's mood. Peering apprehensively inside, I was relieved to see no bloody paw prints, no mud, no smashed furniture. Chris had been busy.

Then I heard panting, and Toby loped awkwardly around the corner, grinning from ear to ear but obviously favoring his front paws, which were encased in a pair of white socks. He pushed his head against my legs, eager for my love. It was nice to have been missed.

I bent down, rubbing his back and dropping kisses on the top of his head. He nuzzled my purse, sniffing out the pepperoni stick. I brought it out, tore open the packaging, and held a chunk of meat out to him. "You see?" I said as he inhaled it. "When I go away, Toby gets a treat. It's okay if I go away, because I bring back special treats. Understand? Good boy!"

Toby nudged my purse with his snout, searching for more. "Ahem."

I looked up to find Chris, arms crossed, staring down at me through his small-framed glasses. I noticed how nicely he was ageing—not a strand of gray in his dirty blond hair. I smiled. "Hi, honey. I missed you. You're looking as gorgeous as ever."

He didn't seem to think so highly of me at that moment. "Charmaine, what are you doing? That's one dog who doesn't deserve any positive attention right now. He needs to know he's in trouble. I've spent the last three hours cleaning his mess."

"I know, Chris, but—"

"What is that? Pepperoni? He's not even supposed to have that. Char, you can't reward him for being terrible!"

Toby got between us, licking his chops, then dashed off and returned with a stuffed animal: a rabbit, which he began tossing in the air, trying to get us to look at him. *Hey, guys! Everyone's home, let's have some fun!*

"I just want him to know we love him," I said.

"If you'd seen what he did today, you wouldn't love him. I, for one, do not feel the slightest, smallest, tiniest bit of love for him."

I tightened my lips. "Maybe that's the problem. Maybe he knows you haven't fallen in love with him yet."

Christopher didn't even look at me. He just stared balefully at Toby.

But I realized I'd found the crux of the problem. Toby didn't misbehave because he was withdrawing from Prozac or because he was a four-legged teenager; he misbehaved because he was uncomfortable living with a man who only tolerated him. Chris had been blaming me for Toby being in our lives and making things increasingly difficult, when all along, it was his fault that Toby couldn't settle in and be a normal, good dog.

Toby looked at Chris, noted his expression, and moaned softly.

"He's gone," Christopher said quietly. "Too much trouble. Count me out. I'm giving up on him. I'm calling the shelter tomorrow and telling them we're bringing him in." He held up a hand before I could speak. "It's no use trying to talk me out of it, Char; my mind is made up. I gave him a chance, more of a chance than anyone else would have given him. But I told you years ago, I don't want to spend my life dealing with kids, and that's what this is like. We should have sent him back months ago. I do not want to hear a word about it."

This sounded like a much-rehearsed speech. I stared, stunned, at Christopher's retreating back.

The stuffed rabbit flew at my chest. Toby sat at my feet, quaking with energy. I sighed and rebuttoned my coat. "I'm taking him for a walk," I called to Chris. "You need a break. And Toby needs some exercise. . . . Let's go, you little brat. You've really gotten yourself in trouble this time. Chris is mad at you, and because of you he's mad at me, and because he's mad at me, I'm mad at you!"

The evening was cool and the sky clear, an endless vista of stars. Even with his paws bandaged and wrapped in socks, Toby was thrilled to be out walking. Watching him lift his big, beautiful head to sniff the breeze, I realized that although he might be gone tomorrow, he was here tonight. And that meant I still had a chance to influence Chris. "You're lucky you have me on your side, big guy," I said.

He sat in front of me on the cold sidewalk, looked up, and lifted a paw. *Peace?*

I couldn't help but laugh. "What on earth am I going to do with you, Toby?"

I wasn't laughing when I got home. I was still upset that Christopher wanted to send our new dog away and disappointed with myself for not being able to help Toby adjust to his new life. So I retreated to the bedroom. Toby, probably sensing that Chris didn't want him around, followed at my heels.

Inside the bedroom, I turned to face him. "Toby, I think that rather than hiding behind me, you ought to be upstairs kissing up to Chris. 'Cause if you don't score some points fast, you're going to be history come morning."

Toby stared at me. *Seriously?*

"You know how Chris is," I said. "If things aren't perfect, they're no good at all. Well, you're not perfect, so we'll just have to get rid of you!" My voice had risen. Toby swiveled his head toward the door. *Hey, Char, keep it down.*

I lowered my voice. "It's a good thing Chris and I never had kids. One temper tantrum and they'd be off to the orphanage. Chris standing there saying, 'Take him, please, Sister Frances. This kid refuses to sleep on cue, won't eat his peas and spinach, and cries when I'm trying to think. He's yours. He doesn't fit into my routine, so I'm giving him away.'"

"Charmaine . . . that's a bit much, don't you think?"

I wheeled to see Chris standing in the doorway.

"Is that really how you see me?" he asked quietly.

"I don't know. I guess so." My shoulders slumped. "Well, not really. I just don't understand how you could . . . give up on Toby like this. Life isn't always perfect, Christopher."

"Don't you think I know that? I've tried hard with Toby, and you know it. But this is just dumb. Toby needs . . . I don't know what he needs. Which is exactly the problem."

"But we can figure it out if we—"

Christopher held up his hand. "Dooks never behaved like this. Never. When he *did* misbehave, we corrected him, and he didn't do the same thing the very next day. Isn't that right?"

"Yes, but Chris, Dooks also used to take off every time he wasn't on a leash. Think how often we had to chase him all over the neighborhood. And what about the havoc he wreaked during thunderstorms?"

"He wasn't that bad. Certainly not like Toby. If we're going to have another dog, I want one like Dooks. I do *not* want one like *him*."

"I know Toby's destructive, Chris. I know he is. But he's also the most sweet and loving dog I've ever known, even including Dooks. That's why he always wants to be around us. He sits at my feet while I'm working on the computer, walks with me to the mailbox, puts his head in my lap when I lie down to read the paper . . ."

"I know, but—"

"No matter what you think of him, he loves *us*. He's happiest when he's with one of us, but he's most in bliss when we're all together."

"But we can't always be together, Char. That's the problem."

"What about the neighborhood kids? They adore him, and he's affectionate and gentle with them no matter what. He never gets aggressive, even when they climb on him or pull his tail."

Chris ran a hand through his hair. "Fine, have the neighborhood kids pay for the next batch of toilet tank lids."

"Haven't you noticed how Toby takes care of his stuffed animals? He carries them around the house and sleeps with them; he licks them to clean them; he cares for them like a litter of pups."

"Exactly. He takes care of his *own* stuff, but has no problem destroying *ours*. Wouldn't you like to be able to go out for the evening without worrying that we'll come back to find our furniture rearranged and all the books knocked off the shelves?"

"Yes, of course, but don't you see? It doesn't always happen, so Toby's not wantonly destructive. We just need to reinforce his good qualities."

"How?"

I opened my mouth. Closed it.

"I'm going to watch the news," Chris said, and left the room.

Alone with Toby, I picked up a picture that sat on our dresser: a white German Shepard on the beach in front of our summer cottage, gazing calmly at the camera. Dooks.

It was true that Dooks had left Toby with big shoes—or paw prints—to fill. He had been named as a joke after my husband—Christopher John Dooks Alcock—because

Chris and I didn't have children to carry on the family name. And for the eleven years we had had Dooks, he had truly been a member of the family; that was why it had taken us so long to even consider getting another dog.

So now we had Toby . . . but perhaps not for much longer. If Christopher had his way, there would never be a photo of a big, grinning Chesapeake Bay retriever to accompany the portrait of Dooks on the dresser.

And what could I say? Chris had a point. To a large extent, in the last couple of months our lives had been reduced to cleaning up after Toby, worrying about Toby, arguing about Toby. Each time we discovered a new mess, we'd stand, stunned, in the doorway of whatever room had been emptied, damaged, or rearranged, asking ourselves and each other what we could possibly do next. Neither of us could come up with a good answer. Toby had invaded our home, our privacy, and our private lives. Now, instead of cuddling in bed at night, sharing our hopes and dreams, my husband and I lay there discussing Toby.

In short, this dog was becoming not a beloved member of our family, but a liability in our marriage. Was the love I felt for him worth the wedge he was driving between me and my husband?

Toby rested his head on my lap and gazed at me with his brown and yellow eyes. *Don't be mad.* I stroked his silky hair, lingering on the little waves on his neck and shoulders. "What got into you today, Toby? This one was pretty bad. This one was the worst. What the heck happened?"

He just sighed.

Seven

Expert Advice

"What do you think set Toby off yesterday?" I asked Chris at the breakfast table.

"Set him off? Is that what you call what he did—being 'set off'?"

Okay, so my husband was still furious—but I actually found his answer encouraging. At least he hadn't said, "Who cares? We're getting rid of the big lug today, so it doesn't matter what he does or why he does it." There might still be a chance for Toby, if only I could give Christopher some reason to hope. . . .

"Maybe he was upset with us about something," I said.

Before Chris could respond, Toby pushed through his dog door, trotted over to me in his stocking feet, and dropped a slobbery stuffed animal on my lap. A peace offering.

"Thanks, Toby. Unfortunately, your gifts don't make up for the problems you cause."

"That's for sure," Chris grunted. "And by the way, why would *he* be upset with *us?*"

"Actually, I thought about that all night. And, well, we *were* warned he has separation anxiety . . ."

"Yesterday was hardly the first time you've been gone overnight, Char."

"No, but you know as well as I do that Toby's been getting . . . well, worse . . . about being left alone. That's why I tried packing my suitcase for my trip while he was in the backyard."

"But he caught you at it."

"Yes." Toby had wandered into the bedroom while I was distracted by a phone call—and fixed his gaze on my open suitcase. For a moment he'd nudged my clothes and toiletries around with his nose, then he turned and gave me the biggest, saddest stare I had ever seen—even for Toby. While I finished packing, he kept climbing into the suitcase and standing on my clothes; afterward he followed me into the garage, where I had to drag him physically out of the car. "He caught me trying to leave, Christopher. It traumatized him. Doesn't that affect the way you feel about him?"

"Wait. You're telling me I should be *more* understanding with Toby because he's getting *worse?*"

I chose to sidestep that one; better to focus on actions instead of feelings. "How was he after I left yesterday? Did you keep to the routine before you went to work, like we discussed?"

"Routines" were part of our plan to treat Toby like a bright child. We had heard that children like consistency, so we had implemented strict schedules and activities for Toby. We had developed a routine for his exercise, a routine for meal times, and a routine before either of us left the house. We even had routines for the use of commands, making sure we used exactly the same words and tones to give instructions like "wait," "take it," and "stay." And it had worked. That was the thing. For a while, Chris and I had been able to leave the house for five minutes and return to find clothing still in the closets, furniture still upright, nothing broken.

But now . . . this.

"Oh, I stuck to the routine," Chris said. "Absolutely. I took him for a walk, made sure he had food, water, and toys, and told him to guard the house, like we used to do with Dooks."

"Did he listen?"

"How would I know that, Char?"

"Because he listened before."

"Almost everything we've tried works for a *while*."

I hesitated, then took the plunge. "Last night you said you don't love him. Maybe . . . maybe he can tell. Maybe he's acting out to get your attention."

"And maybe he's ready to enroll at MIT and study rocket science. Come on, Charmaine. Toby's smart, but he's not *that* smart. Besides, you've got it backward. I thought he was a great dog until all this started."

I couldn't argue with that. "Okay . . . but still, there's something about us *leaving* that seems to drive him crazy. So his behavior yesterday, maybe that was his way of saying 'I'm warning you, if you leave me alone, I'll rip your house apart.'"

"Since he's so smart, why doesn't he just write that on a note and stick it on the fridge?"

"Or maybe he's afraid that when we leave we'll never come back, like when his first owner died. Or maybe he's bored and looking for something to do. Or maybe—"

"Or maybe he's insane."

"Chris . . ." I said, but the truth was, my husband had just articulated my greatest fear. I was worried about Toby's mental health. Despite his loveable qualities, I couldn't disagree that last night marked a new high for destructive behavior. Our relationship with Toby had become a kind of arms race. He would do something unpredictable and destructive; we would adjust; he would do something different. For example, our response to his habit of shutting himself into rooms while we were gone and then tearing them apart was to put him in the living room before we departed, then close all the doors into other rooms. At least Toby hadn't extended his skill with faucet handles to doorknobs.

Still, this approach didn't help for long. Free to roam the rest of the house, Toby simply tipped over our standing candlestick holders, the footstool, or anything else that got in his way.

When it came to unpredictability, our dog was always one step ahead of us.

Or maybe we still weren't thinking about this the right way.

I thought back to the exchange I'd had with the gas station clerk on my trip home to Calgary. Maybe Chris and I had been wrong to treat Toby like a bright child. Now that I thought about it, he seemed more like an unruly teenager, uncertain of his place in the world and throwing temper tantrums when he didn't get his way. Or maybe he was going through some kind of withdrawal from the Prozac; maybe he was a drug-addled teenager, acting out because his parents no longer let him get his fix.

From this perspective, I had to wonder if Christopher and I weren't the ones at fault. Maybe we needed to set more defined limits for Toby, to be more clear about our expectations, to establish a system of consequences and rewards—just as the parents of adolescent children do.

The problem was, I didn't know that much about being a parent, even though I had worked with hundreds of kids in my years as a correctional officer, youth worker, and manager of custody facilities for young offenders. During that period I had dealt with many teenagers who had, for various reasons, ended up in detention centers, group homes, or other facilities. Most of these kids were considered bad apples, but "trainable."

I had preferred to think of them as works in progress. Together, my colleagues and I developed behavioral modification programs for these youths, programs that had helped many of the young people grow and change during their time with us. Of course, what we tried didn't always work; inevitably there were kids who, for whatever reason, seemed destined to stay on a destructive path.

Like Toby.

I scratched his ears. "Chris?"

My husband looked up from his coffee. "Uh-oh. Here it comes."

"Remember that boy, Brian, I told you about when I was a youth worker?"

"The one you thought had such a bright future?"

"That's right." Brian had been one of my more heart-breaking cases back then. As a young teenager, he had spent too much time with the wrong crowd and ended up incarcerated for a variety of petty crimes. That was a common enough story, unfortunately; but two things had set Brian apart from the other young men in my care: first, under his tough exterior he was a real softie; and second, he had dreams that reached beyond the schemes common to most future prison inmates. He was also an exceptional athlete, who on the field became a different boy—became *himself*, a teenager full of team spirit and quick with a smile. Watching him play, I would think, *This kid is going places.*

"Is this also the Brian who ended up in jail," Christopher said. He had already guessed where I was going with my story.

But I was not to be dissuaded. "Yes, he did end up in jail, but that's my point: he wasn't the only one at fault. If a kid with behavior problems is going to change, he needs things at home to change, too. That means getting the parents involved. *Both* parents. But sometimes that doesn't happen. Sometimes one parent just isn't interested or is burned out. Brian's father actually *wanted* Brian to be put in an institution so he wouldn't have to deal with him anymore."

"What about the mother?"

"She worked with us for a while, but when things went from bad to worse, she was forced to choose between her son and her husband. She chose her husband."

Christopher stared at me, stony faced.

"My point is, Brian's parents gave up on their son, their family . . . they gave up on love. So Brian gave up, too. But it didn't have to work out that way. Brian had a lot of potential. He could have been a wonderful man if his parents had only been on his side."

Christopher shifted his gaze to Toby, whose tail thumped the floor once. *Listen to her.* Chris sighed. "Char, we've gotten advice from every dog expert in Alberta, professional or amateur. Exactly what do you propose we do?"

I felt my heart leap, but kept the excitement off my face. I knew this was a reprieve at best. If I couldn't come up with an answer to Christopher's question—a *good* answer— he would go right back to insisting that Toby vanish from our home.

Besides, he was right. Advice had proven easy to come by: "Toby may just be adjusting to his new surroundings and learning how to be home alone; give it a bit more time," said one trainer. "Make sure he knows you're the pack leader, be firm," said another. "Try the clicker, it always helps with barking," insisted a third.

Still, I was heartened. "What we need is a better understanding of Toby," I said. "Not just misbehaving dogs in general but *Toby:* where he came from and what kinds of things worked with him in the past."

"Putting him in a kennel worked for Dave and Yasmin."

"Yeah, because there were other dogs in there with him. It's being alone he can't stand. In fact . . . I wonder if he's *ever* really been alone. Maybe his original owners never went anywhere without him."

"We could call the old lady and ask."

"Wait . . . wait a minute. We don't have to do that. I just remembered; when David gave us Toby's bag of stuff, there was a letter from Toby's original owner in there. She wrote it to the rescue agency when she gave Toby up."

"I never saw that. What does it say?"

"Well . . . I only sort of skimmed it myself the day we brought Toby home. Then I forgot all about it." I shot to my feet. "I'll go read it now."

Toby followed me out of the room.

I found the letter on the top shelf of the bedroom closet. Sitting on the floor with Toby's head in my lap, I unfolded the pages. Toby's eyes twitched with attention. *Got some good news?*

"All right, Tobes, let's see if there are any clues in this letter to let us know why you're such a jerk sometimes. Before I start, is there anything you want to come clean about?"

He licked my hand.

"So your response is to pre-kiss me. That's not a good sign. Okay, let's see . . ."

The four-page letter, in neat and precise handwriting, had clearly come from the heart and was full of love and sadness at having to give Toby away. The author started with all the things Toby could do: sit, stay, sit pretty, shake a paw, lie down, come, talk quiet.

I chuckled. We had seen Toby respond quickly to commands, showing off the polite and well-trained Jekyll who coexisted with the havoc-wreaking Hyde. "It says you can do basic things, Toby. Now let's see if we can find the part about 'can also be a monster.'"

Toby licked my other hand.

I read about the food he enjoyed, how he loved to be cuddled and scratched, and the fact that he knew the names of all his toys. "Why is it that you like that stuffed pink rabbit so much, Toby? It's a bit weird, you know. But the 'loves being cuddled and scratched' part, I get. Even a grown dog loves that." I scratched his neck as I read on. His eyes closed.

Much of the information came as no surprise: we knew Toby loved to be with people. We knew he loved to run head-on into a stream of water coursing from a garden hose; we knew this made him bark and attempt to slurp a drink.

Then I encountered a glimmer of the insight I was looking for: When he is stressed, he may lock himself in the bathroom or other small rooms, paw at you and try climbing on you, or hide behind furniture or push at lamps, etc., to get your attention.

"Oh boy, Toby. Oh, man, I should have paid closer attention to this letter the first time. You really fooled us, acting so well-behaved at the foster home."

Toby's eyebrows twitched.

"You might as well go pack your bags, because you know Chris is going to use this letter as proof-positive that you're incorrigible *and* untrainable. For your sake, I hope what they say about teaching an old dog new tricks isn't true."

Next, insight became advice. The letter cautioned us to close all bathroom, bedroom, and laundry room doors before leaving the house because, if Toby heard a loud noise and got scared, he would close himself into a room, panic when he couldn't get out, and . . .

"It says here you might 'possibly cause damage.' Now there's a surprise. I'll bet Chris is calling the rescue agency right now for that very reason."

Reading on, it struck me how often the previous owner mentioned that Toby was easily stressed and that stress caused him to misbehave. I didn't know what kinds of things had gone on in her house, but what could possibly be causing him stress *here?*

"What stresses you, Toby? Because to be honest, as far as I can see—and I know Chris would agree—the only source of stress in this house is *you.*"

In response, Toby wagged his tail. *I can't help it.* Oh, how I wished he could really speak.

As the letter progressed, it became increasingly clear that Toby's previous owners had treated him differently from how we did in numerous ways. They had allowed him to lounge on furniture and sleep on their bed. Neither of these behaviors was allowed in our home, although we knew Toby sometimes crawled onto the couch and over-stuffed chairs when we weren't looking. Either we would walk out of the office to find him sprawled on the couch, taking an afternoon siesta, or we would find telltale dog hairs that told us he had taken advantage of our absence to enjoy a comfy rest on the downstairs sofa.

Like a worried parent, I began to second-guess myself. Was Toby stressed in our home because he couldn't sleep in an overstuffed chair or on the bed with Chris and me? If so . . . a chair, well, maybe. The bed, no way. Not in my wildest dreams could I imagine us making room in our bed for ninety pounds of snoring retriever. Although there had been a few nights when storms passed through, and we awoke to find Toby snoring loudly between Chris and me. We hadn't even noticed our sneaky dog climbing up to safety.

Every word in the letter verified that Toby had *always* had quirky habits and had *always* been a bit of a trouble-maker. So why had the previous owners put up with his behavior? I guess that didn't matter. It was up to Christopher and me—or whoever got Toby next, if it came to that—to change him.

But the goodness I saw in Toby when I looked into his warm eyes also shone through in the letter. "'Toby is a sensitive and most loving creature,'" I read aloud. "'And he has a special gift of intuition and insight.' Well, that's good, Toby; it means you already know your days with us are numbered if you don't give up your wayward habits."

The letter held other clues to understanding this dog. For instance, it corroborated what Yasmin had told us about how Toby had alerted his previous owner that her husband had passed away.

I scratched his ears. "Oh, Toby, that's so sad. How did you alert her, exactly? Did you just lie down beside your dad, or did you go and bark to get mom's attention?"

Toby looked at me, head on his front paws, and sighed deeply. *Don't ask.*

"You still miss him, don't you?" I rubbed him, knowing that probably he was still grieving—there was a good possibility he had never gotten over that death; maybe he was still experiencing depression as he waited in vain for one of his favorite people to return. Could that be the real reason behind his days of destruction?

The letter also revealed the emotions of its writer, the woman who had lost her husband and was about to give up a beloved family member as well. Her words were tender, and she talked about Toby as though he were a child. It reminded me of the many heartfelt letters I had read from birth mothers written to the children they had given up. The words came from a place of selfless loving, and that love shone through as they explained their gut-wrenching decision to place a child, their own flesh and blood, up for adoption.

In some ways, Toby's original mom had done the same thing: given this dog, whom she loved, to a family better able to care for him than she was at that point in her life. A selfless act. I felt for her, too.

I looked at Toby, curled up at my feet, looking serene and content. I could picture him lying like this day after day, missing his previous owners and unable to understand that they were, to him, gone forever.

I realized I'd just had an epiphany.

"You lost your favorite person in the world, and you still miss him, isn't that right?" I wrapped my arms around Toby, burying my face in his warm neck. "Are you still waiting for him and his wife to come for you, Tobes? Are you just putting up with Chris and me until your real owners return? Are you getting frustrated? Is that it?"

Toby licked my hand and then my face. This time I wasn't sure what he meant—but I hoped it wasn't *That's right. Sorry, but you'll never be acceptable substitutes.*

"You poor thing. What would it do to you if we give you away now? You've been here for more than half a year; this is your home now. You'd end up grieving for your old owners *and* us!"

Full of new conviction, I shot to my feet. I needed to convince Christopher that Toby deserved another chance. He wasn't a bad dog; quite the opposite—he was so loyal and attached to his previous owners that he couldn't settle into living with us. That was admirable, not pathological.

"Toby," I said, "people could learn a lot from you. You

know the meaning of commitment. You know it means never giving up on someone. I'm just so sorry you can't understand that those people are gone forever, and you don't have to wait for them anymore."

I strode off to find Chris. Surely, what I had just realized would convince him to change his mind about getting rid of Toby. After all, if anyone knew the power of commitment, it was Christopher.

Commitment had saved his life.

Eight

Rescue Me

When Chris and I were young, we had a tumultuous relationship. We'd met in Ontario, our home province, when I was just eighteen. Chris, eight years older than I, was easygoing without being irresponsible, a refreshing change from guys my own age. He was also good looking, a deep thinker, and a great dancer. In high school, he had been a competitive diver, tennis player, and sailor, and he still had the body to show for it.

We were attracted to one another instantly and very soon found that being together was pretty much the most fun either of us had ever had. Chris understood me in a way no one else ever had; sometimes, I swore he could read my mind. We enjoyed the same things: being outdoors, great food, talking about our dreams for hours on end.

Well, actually, I did most of the talking; Christopher was the quiet one in our relationship. He introduced me to sailing, and I introduced him to the pleasures of long walks, daydreaming, and dancing under the stars.

But we were young and unsure about locking ourselves into a relationship when there was so much world, and so many other people, to explore. We also had the self-centeredness of youth, and lacked the tools to overcome disagreements in a way that let us both win and come to a better understanding of each other. During seven years of dating, we broke up and got back together 101 times, probably driving our family and friends to distraction.

Then on Valentine's Day, after a period of long-distance dating, Christopher came back to Ontario from his new home in Alberta and asked me what I thought about moving out there with him. Six months later, I happily made the move. I felt we'd both grown up, and, although we weren't ready to say "I do" for a lifetime, we were definitely ready to take our relationship to a new level.

I'm not sure we would have ever reached the point of marriage if we hadn't gone through an incident that changed everything.

It was a late summer day in 1994, and Chris and I were on Lac La Biche, a large, cold body of water in Alberta, Canada, sailing our sixteen-foot Hobie Cat catamaran. Speeding across the glittering blue waters of the lake, we were exhilarated, having the time of our young lives.

The Hobie was built for exhilaration. It had a mast thirty feet tall, holding a multicolored mainsail and a jib sail bulging with wind. On a Hobie, you sit not in a cockpit but on a taut black mesh surface called the "trampoline." The trampoline is secured between the two bright-yellow pontoons shaped like bananas.

As the wind shifted and Chris prepared to turn the boat, he called, "Ready to come about!" I slid across the trampoline to the far side as the boom brought the mainsail around. I then pulled Chris as close as I could for a kiss, breathing in his fresh, summer smell. My Chris. He had been sailing since he was fourteen years old, and I trusted him with my life.

"You warm enough?" he asked. Surprisingly, I was. Usually I got cold on the boat, where the wind off the water made the air feel much cooler than it did on the beach. But this day the wind was warm enough to wear just a T-shirt under my life jacket. The wind was also very strong. "I can't believe how fast we're going! I could water-ski behind the boat."

"Better than that," Chris said, "put on the harness."

The trapeze harness is like a diaper you pull on over your clothing, with a line running from it to the top of the mast. Part of the fun of sailing a Hobie is putting on the harness and hiking out onto one of the pontoons, then leaning backward over the water. Ultimately, you're speeding along with your body dangling over the lake by a line attached to a clip at your waist, with only your toes in contact with the boat. It feels amazing . . . as long as the captain of the boat is someone you trust.

I trusted Chris, of course, but . . . "We're going pretty fast. Do you think I'll be okay?"

"Sure you will. It'll be a blast. Go for it."

I climbed into the harness and made my way onto the pontoon, then leaned backward away from the boat,

connected only by my tippy toes. Butterflies of excitement tickled my stomach as the water hissed past just
beneath me. Chris made a small adjustment with the
rudder, and suddenly I was rising into the air along with
the pontoon until Chris judged I was high enough and
adjusted the rudder again. Now, with only one pontoon
in the water, we were flying over the lake faster than
ever. "Wow!" I yelled over the humming of the rigging.

Then, without warning, the wind surged. The pontoon
in the water dug into the lake, causing the Hobie to "pitchpole." In an instant, the boat turned from a racing shadow
to a careening mass of aluminum and sailcloth. When the
violence ended, I found myself suspended upside-down just
above the water. I had a vague memory of bashing into the
mast, but I didn't feel any serious injuries. Still, I couldn't
get out of the harness no matter how I thrashed. Nor could
I see my boyfriend anywhere. "Chris!" I cried. "Chris!" I
swiped water out of my eyes. I was terrified and helpless in
this position. The shoreline wavered in the far distance.
Where was Chris?

Suddenly his arms were around me. "It's okay, Charmaine. You okay?" He sounded so calm, not rattled at all.
There was even a hint of laughter in his voice.

I immediately relaxed. "You didn't do that on purpose,
did you?" I said. I was kidding, although Christopher had
told me that in his youth he used to pitchpole boats for fun.
Hobies are lightweight but strong vessels; they're made to
take abuse. Besides, Chris as always told me, "The best sailing is minutes before the storm."

"That's what you get for taking the last of the coffee this
morning," Chris said. Then he kissed me and helped me

get out of the harness. Within minutes, he had expertly righted the boat.

"My hero!" I said. Although we'd only been in the water for about ten minutes, I was already cold. He told me to climb onto the boat first, but when I tried, I discovered I didn't have the strength to haul my body weight up. Chris swam over to help me, and, just as he reached out to boost me up, another gust caught the sail, shoving the boat forcefully away from us. Clutching the pontoon post, I was dragged along, away from Chris. He grabbed for my leg, but the boat was already moving too fast. He struck out, swimming after us. I heard him yelling for me to stay with the boat, so I clung to the post with all my strength.

When the wind finally died down a little, I turned to look for Chris and saw nothing but a vast, blank expanse of gray water. Overhead, clouds obscured the sun; even the birds seemed to have abandoned the area. "Chris!" I shouted.

My arms ached. I was having trouble hanging on, and I couldn't do anything to turn the boat to the wind and slow it down. In fact, the wind picked up again, and as the boat surged, I was torn from the post.

I watched the Hobie's colorful sails gliding off toward the far side of the lake, some seven miles away. Within moments, it formed only a tiny spot on the water. I was probably half a mile away from Chris, who no doubt thought I was still with the boat.

Alone in the middle of the vast lake, I was gripped by fear such as I had never before known. The water was choppy and cold, waves slapping me repeatedly in the face. The wind moaned, and I started shivering.

"Chris!" The wind's howl was the only response. I was truly alone, a tiny speck floating under a wide gray sky. No signs of life in any direction. But I had to do something, so I turned and swam toward the part of the lake where I'd last seen Christopher. With every stroke, I yelled for Chris—or for help.

At first, swimming was good. It gave me something to focus on and restored my mental strength. "Charmaine," I said to myself, "don't you know that crying will get you nowhere? Here's what you're going to do. You're going to find Chris, and you're going to cover him with kisses and tell him you love him. Then the two of you are going to get out of this mess together. I don't know how. But you are. So just keep swimming."

Whitecaps worked to push me further into the lake. Exhausted, I began treading water. Then something caught my eye: an arm, waving above the chop. Christopher! I waved back as hard as I could. He swam toward me. Everything would be all right now. Christopher would save me.

Relieved, excited, exhausted, I clung to Chris the moment he reached me, feasting my eyes on him. He took my face in both hands. "Did you do that on purpose?"

I laughed. "That's what you get for flipping the boat on me."

"Okay, here are our options. We could huddle up and drift across to the other shore, but it's farmland over there, and I think about seven miles away. That's a long way to drift. Or we could head toward the campground. I figure we're about four miles away from there, and we know there are people there."

I was immediately reassured by his confident tone. "Let's go for the sure thing."

"I agree, unless you're too tired or cold."

"No, let's do it."

Thinking back, this choice seems crazy. Wouldn't we have been better off conserving our energy, huddling up for warmth, and drifting until we reached shore or were found? Maybe. But I think we both knew we had to choose action over drifting, to fight for life rather than simply hope for the best. Even alone and adrift, we wanted to exert some control over our lives. So we swam because we could, and as long as we could, we would.

At first, reenergized by our reunion, we found swimming fairly easy, but soon each stroke became a chore. We varied our strokes—crawl, breaststroke, backstroke—to rest some of our muscles. Soon my entire body was numb, and my lungs strained for air. When Christopher turned to smile at me, his lips were purple, and I knew mine must be, too.

We knew what we were up against. Even in late August, the water temperature in northern Alberta is quite low; hypothermia can occur after a short period of time, and eventually it will kill you. As minutes turned into hours, and the sky grew darker with storm clouds, I began to realize we weren't going to make it. I stopped swimming, sobbing into the wind as lightning cracked the sky above us. Christopher stroked back to me.

"Char, we can't stop now," he yelled over the storm. "If we stop, we're dead. Come on."

"It's no use! We're still so far from shore. . . . I won't make it, Chris. I won't!" I wanted to tell him to go without me, but I couldn't do it—I didn't want to die alone.

"You have to keep going, Char! You have to! I know you're tired, but we're almost to shore. Okay? We're almost there, sweetheart. Come on. You don't expect me to do this without you, do you? One arm in front of the other. You can do it, Char. That's it . . . that's it . . ."

We went on like that, keeping each other motivated, trying to prevent fear from taking over our minds. After a while, the thunder and lightning stopped and the sky cleared. We took turns pulling one another when we tired. But as I watched Christopher's skin color fade to an unusual shade of blue-gray, my spirits sank. Soon he complained that his muscles were really starting to ache, and he began convulsing and vomiting. The bottom fell out of my stomach.

"Char," he gasped, "I'm starting to cramp up. We need to get help soon."

The thought of Christopher—my rock, my grounding force—losing strength terrified me. Looking toward the beach, I saw bright lights—but they were so far away. . . .

Still, I tried to be encouraging. "Chris, people are looking for us. Look at the beach—there are cars with lights shining out to the water." We began to scream for help again, but our voices were weak and raspy, and we were too far away to be heard. One by one, the cars pulled off, leaving everything still and quiet on shore. As they left, so did all my hope.

Then, in a moment when time seemed to stop, Christopher spoke in a quiet, gentle voice. "Char, I'm cold, and my legs have cramped up. I can't swim anymore. But you've still got some energy, so I'll just float and tread water while you swim for help." I had no idea at the time that he thought he was saying good-bye. He knew he was in grave danger, and he was doing what I had been unable to do for him earlier: sending me to save myself even if it meant he had to die out there alone.

Although I wasn't aware of just how bad his situation was, there was no way I was leaving him. "Chris, I can't. I can't make it to shore without you. Come on. Keep trying."

He smoothed my wet hair out of my eyes and cupped my face with his icy palm. In the middle of all this terror, there was a light in his eyes, a radiant peacefulness that gave me hope again. "I can't. But you can do this, Char. You have to. Because when we get back to shore, we have a wedding to plan."

In that moment I knew I wanted nothing but to spend my life with this man, to fully commit to him and grow old together.

As I gazed at Christopher, maybe for the last time, I finally realized that he was unique and special and the only man for me. "Okay, Chris, I'm going to get help. Promise me you'll stay awake and keep moving. Promise me!"

He promised, and I swam away from him, focusing on only the thing that mattered just then: getting help for Christopher. Negative thoughts I immediately banished. Fighting the terror of swimming alone, I prayed for rescue and silently counted strokes to keep me going.

Every time I paused for breath, I turned to see Christopher floating there in his orange life jacket. Then, after perhaps half an hour, I couldn't see him anymore—not even a speck of orange. Terror gripped me, but my sense of urgency redoubled. I had to trust in myself. I wasn't sure I would make it to shore, but I was sure giving everything I had in the attempt.

Was it because I had fully committed myself to my task, or because Chris had earlier committed himself to me, that a boat appeared at exactly that moment? I will never know. What matters is that it was there, a long way from shore. I called out, waving my arms madly above my head. The boat turned toward me, and at the tiller I saw a teenage boy to whom Chris and I had spoken on the beach that morning. His father was with him, directing him toward me. I wept with joy. They were like angels, sent to save me—save us—just in time.

"Hang on, miss. We'll throw you a line," the man called.

I wanted to get out of the water so badly, but Christopher needed to get out even more. I pointed toward where I had last seen him. "My boyfriend is over there. He can't swim anymore and he may not even be conscious. He's in serious condition. Please, help him."

"We'll be right back!" They left me and went to find Chris. I treaded water for a couple of minutes, then went limp. The relief of being rescued and being reunited with Chris meant I didn't have to fight for my life anymore. So I just floated, waiting. Not soon enough, the boat came back. Father and son, working together, pulled me shaking from the water.

I broke into sobs when I saw Chris lying motionless in the bottom of the boat. I slid over and grabbed his hand. "Chris! I'm here, babe. We'll be on shore soon. Chris, talk to me. . . ." There was no response. His eyes were only partially open, and he was unresponsive to both my voice and my touch. His body was shutting down. Kneeling beside him, I held his cold blue hands and continued to talk to him, soothing him and begging him to hang on.

He didn't seem to know I was there.

Once we reached shore, our rescuers laid Chris on the beach and a couple of people with first aid knowledge began to work on him.

Our rescuer's wife led me away with the suggestion that I find Chris some warm clothes and a hot drink. Only after I had staggered a few yards down the beach did I realize they were not sure Chris was going to make it, and didn't want me there until professional help arrived.

But survive he did!

One year later, Chris and I married, just as he had promised we would. It was a beautiful celebration, a celebration worthy of our vows to always be there for one another.

Lifelines

I wandered into our dimly-lit kitchen to find Chris making himself a sandwich.

"I've been reading that letter from Toby's previous owner," I said. "He depended on them for everything from food to happiness. It made me think back to that day we depended on each other in the lake. What would have happened if we'd given up on one another or didn't trust one another to be there?"

Chris didn't speak, but I could tell by his stillness that he was listening.

"One of the things I've always loved most about you is how you never give up on me," I said. "Sometimes, I think my life started that day in the lake. That was where we learned we could, and would, go the distance for one another. It was what convinced us to get married and stop sitting on the fence. Commitment matters, babe."

A moment passed, then Christopher turned to me and took me in his arms. "You're everything to me," he said. "I love you."

"Me too," I said. "I love that saying, 'Love is what you've been through with someone.'"

"What's the other saying . . . oh, yeah, 'I love you because I know you so well . . . and I love you in spite of knowing you well.'"

"Oh, that's nice. But maybe it means you'll understand this: the reason I'm falling in love with Toby is *because* he's so much work. I know that sounds weird, but it can happen for you, too, if you commit to him like we have to each other. Our rescuers threw us a lifeline that day in the lake. What would have happened if they hadn't? We probably wouldn't be sitting here having this conversation. Well, we're like those people for Toby. We're his lifeline, Chris."

"He is a lot of work," Christopher said in an expressionless voice. "We can say that for sure."

This wasn't the response I wanted. I pressed on. "Remember our wedding? Our vows? We didn't just rattle off a bunch of words; our level of commitment came from the depths of our souls. Because that day in the lake, we realized what it would be like to be without each other."

"I could never be without you," he said.

"It's how I feel, too. And it's what I want Toby to feel from both of us. I want us to go the distance with this dog. When I watch him around people, there's something about him . . . people always tell me it feels like Toby can see into their souls, like he knows something about them they might not even know about themselves. There's something going on with him, Chris, other than the weird behaviors and the destructiveness; I just haven't figured it out yet. What do you say? Are you willing to give him another chance?"

Christopher surprised me with a warm laugh. "I should have known where you were going with all this."

I pressed on. "We're problem solvers, you and I. We can figure this out. And we're not quitters. We make things work better. Do you get what I'm saying?"

Nails clicked on the floor behind me, and Toby gave a soft woof. He sat a few feet away, his gaze bouncing from Christopher to me and back again, as if he knew his future hinged on this moment.

Chris stared at him, then turned and wrapped me in a big hug. "All right. You've convinced me. If you want Toby to stay, he stays. We'll make this work . . . somehow."

"Really?"

"Absolutely." He turned to Toby. "You hear that? You can stay. But you've got to work with us, got it?"

Toby wagged his tail so hard his body vibrated. *Yeah yeah yeah . . .*

"Chris," I said, "remember how I told you I knew Toby was trainable? I've been experimenting. Watch this."

I went and got one of Toby's favorite treats and his white stuffed rabbit. Setting the rabbit on the floor in front of him, I gave the command "Leave it," just as the dog training video had instructed. Toby looked at the rabbit, then at me. *Are you serious?*

"Toby, leave it."

I guess you are. He left it.

"Good boy!" I beamed at Christopher. "You see? He

catches on so quickly. This is way easier than I thought it would be."

Chris gave a soft snort. "But, Charmaine, how is that going to work when you're not here to give the command?"

Ten

Modified

With the help of dog-training books and television programs, I devised a behavioral modification training program for Toby. First, reasoning that more exercise would keep him from getting so wound up when left home alone, I scheduled him for not one but two walks a day, the first in the morning before I left and the second in the afternoon when I got home. Double walks, together with evening trips to the off-leash dog park and games of fetch in the yard, should wear out even the most energetic dog. But just in case, whenever possible I also began playing games with Toby throughout the day. Hide and seek, which we called "find it," became Toby's favorite pastime during television commercials.

True to his word, Christopher joined in. Together we

started teaching Toby commands we wanted him to know. In addition to "leave it," he quickly picked up "wait," "quiet," "excellent," and "sshhhh." I knew that praise was important, so when I caught him being good, I made a point of showering him with compliments and affection. "Good boy!" I'd yodel when Toby charged through the kitchen and out the dog door without stepping in his water bowl. I knew I was going a bit overboard—I swear Christopher and Toby sometimes exchanged looks of disbelief—but I was determined to help Toby change, no matter the cost.

Another of my goals was to help Toby stop being so anxious about loud or unfamiliar noises. One video suggested helping your dog overcome such fears by doing something the animal enjoys at the same time the noise is occurring. I combined fetch and vacuuming . . . but unfortunately this did not put an end to Toby's fear of the vacuum's roar. Instead, whenever Toby felt like playing, he dropped piles of toys in front of the vacuum.

A few days into the new plan, Christopher broke ranks in order to get some housework done, pushing the toys aside so he could start the vacuum cleaner. Rebuffed, Toby gave Chris a look we knew all too well and ran from the room. "Three, two, one . . ." I said, and heard Toby rattle the shower door. Chris turned off the vacuum. A moment later, I heard the click of the bathroom door closing.

As always, Toby looked overjoyed when I let him out. I squatted in front of him. "Can't you tell we love you when we play with you and pet you and feed you and walk you? Isn't that enough? Do you really need us to rescue you, too?"

Toby just wagged his tail.

The big problem was that no matter what we did, Toby

continued to wreak havoc in the house when we left him alone. Not every time, but far too often. If we made the mistake of leaving the bathroom door open when we left the house, as soon as we returned we'd find ourselves heading to Home Depot for yet another toilet tank lid.

"He's taken the boot and shoe racks right off the wall," Christopher told me one day when I got home from work. He pointed to a row of holes in the wall.

"You mean he ripped the screws all the way out this time?" I asked.

"Yes. The front hall is a mess; shoes and drywall shavings everywhere. Look, he's knocked the table over, as well, and just missed breaking the window in the front entrance hallway. I'm amazed the floor didn't crack."

"Well, that's not so bad . . ."

Christopher knew what I was trying to do. "This isn't working, Char," he said, as he carried the antique wooden table that had sat in our front entrance for years toward the garage, where Toby couldn't damage it. "Why are we always rearranging our lives for Toby?"

He had a point, of course. He and I had always enjoyed a flexible and independent lifestyle, but now. . . . It was at times like this that I was sorely tempted to let Christopher have his way and send Toby back to where he'd come from.

Toby squeezed up to the window beside me and craned his neck straight ahead. I looked out, too. Chris was in the garage where he couldn't be seen, and there was nothing out of the ordinary out there. A few dry leaves skittered across the frozen ground.

Spotting a big black raven on a lamppost, Toby barked and looked at me proudly: *I see it too, Mom!*

I laughed. "Toby, you goof. I was looking at my peaceful past, not that bird. But you're right: might as well look at what's really out there."

A few days later, after returning from work to find shoes, boots, yoga mats, hats, mittens, and coats covering the front hall, Christopher suggested installing a nanny cam. "Maybe we'll get an idea of what's going on in his head if we see him in action."

I thought this was a great idea . . . assuming it worked. But I said, "Knowing Toby, he'll probably figure out a way to turn the camera off." More and more, our dog reminded me of the kids I had worked with as a correctional worker and family mediator: always trying to outsmart the staff, the system, and their parents. Maybe getting an older dog hadn't been such a good idea after all. Instead of a puppy, we'd ended up with a rebellious adolescent.

Before leaving for work the next morning, we set up the new camera, pointing it at Toby's favorite hall closet . . . and came home to another disaster in the hallway. And the camera captured nothing. Toby hadn't needed to outsmart us; we hadn't turned the camera on.

The next day, we set it up again and this time made sure to switch it on. Christopher fixed the camera to a chair so it wouldn't be knocked over and broken. Toby looked from the camera to us, then over at the closet. I could practically hear his brain working over the new situation. He cocked an eyebrow and one ear at me: *You can't catch me.*

He was a perfect angel that day.

Two days later, he emptied the basement shelves instead of the closet under surveillance.

As we cleaned up the mess, Toby walked up and

dropped a toy at our feet. Chris kicked it aside and kept working. "Christopher," I said, "he's just trying to make things right. It's his way of apologizing."

"I'd prefer if he said 'Sorry, I'll never do it again.'"

"It's like what you and I do after a hard day or a disagreement."

"I don't believe I've ever brought you a slobbery stuffed animal."

"You know what I mean. It's about forgiveness. Do you know what my mentor at the youth detention facility used to tell me about forgiveness? Forgiveness is 'for giving.' It's a gift you give—to others, but also to yourself."

"Well, thanks to Toby, you and I have been giving ourselves a lot of gifts lately."

"Chris . . ."

"I know, I know, commitment." He sighed and set the last of the books back on the shelf. "Okay, Toby, I forgive you. Just . . . *please* don't do it again."

But Toby did it again. And again. Just not all the time, which was actually part of the problem; there seemed to be no pattern to or reason for his bursts of craziness.

After a few failed attempts with the nanny cam, we gave up and sought professional help instead.

First, we went to our veterinarian. We described our problems with Toby, and I asked if maybe his previous owners had had a good reason for putting him on human Prozac.

Dr. Lyons raised her eyebrows. "Tell me again why Toby's previous owners gave him up."

"Well, he had two elderly owners. The man died, and

Toby found him and went into a deep depression."

"It's not uncommon for dogs to respond that way to a loss, much like humans. But why exactly was he on Prozac?"

"I assume he was medicated to suppress his energy, because he does like to play. When the rescue people got him, he was grossly overweight and underexercised."

Chris broke in. "Or maybe they tried to medicate his behavior problems away."

Dr. Lyons grimaced. "Unfortunately, some veterinarians will write prescriptions when they should be prescribing that the owners take better care of their pets. How much exercise is he getting now?"

"Tons," I said. "Honestly, he gets more exercise than an Olympic athlete in training. But he's still acting up. Do you think he needs the Prozac?"

"No."

Beside me, Christopher sighed loudly. Still, he gave Toby a pat on the back. "What have we gotten ourselves into? Just how deranged are you, Toby?"

"Come on, Chris," I said. "Everyone needs a little help sometimes. In Toby's case, that help was . . . drugs."

Dr. Lyons took Toby's big head in her gentle hands. "Charmaine, Chris, it seems that Toby has some serious challenges. It sounds like he suffers from separation anxiety, which might be causing some of the behavioral problems."

"But what's causing the anxiety?" I asked.

"Who knows? He may have been born prone to anxiety, and life circumstances have only made it worse. It's difficult to tell without having seen him in past surroundings."

"All we know is he went from his original owners, one

of whom died, to a foster home with lots of other dogs, to us."

"That's a lot of change for one worried dog."

"So what can we do?" Chris asked. I shot him a grateful glance.

"Well . . . I can write you a prescription right now, if you want to try the medication route."

Christopher and I looked at each other. I shook my head. Although a holy terror wasn't my idea of the ideal pet, neither was a drugged canine.

"But before we do that," Dr. Lyons said, "I'd first recommend that you speak to an animal behaviorist."

"You mean like a doggy psychologist?" Christopher asked.

"Of sorts. I know one who's wonderful. If anyone can get Toby to change his behavior through training, she can." She handed us a card.

In the car, I read the card to Christopher. "'Good Dog! Effective training for your canine companion. Maggie Schlegl, Animal Behaviorist.' And then her number. No website."

"I don't care if we have to contact her with drums or smoke signals," Christopher said. "Let's just get her on the case. Toby! In the back, please."

Eleven

The Behaviorist

We arranged for Maggie, the behaviorist, to visit our home the following week and see Toby in action. Thinking it would be good to give her as much information as possible, Christopher and I sat down ahead of time to discuss and record some of the more memorable Toby incidents. We hadn't really talked about Toby's antics for a while; it had been too touchy a subject. But this was different.

I brought a pen and pad of paper to the dining table. Christopher set a steaming cup of tea in front of each of us.

The moment we started talking, Toby realized that he was the subject under discussion. He shot a glance in our direction, then rose and stalked off. A few moments later, the bathroom door clicked shut; soon after that, we heard and the slamming noise of the toilet seat bouncing up and down. For a dog who hated loud noises, Toby sure made enough of his own. I said, "I hope he does that when Maggie comes—then she'll know what we're dealing with."

"Let's just ignore him for a while. Okay, where to begin? Oh, remember the time he chased the rabbit in the park? What about the time he almost dove into the hot tub with us? . . ."

I scribbled those down, laughing to myself. "Or the time he came from playing in the cul-de-sac with the neighborhood kids carrying all those toys that weren't his? That deflated beach ball, a stuffed animal, a hockey puck . . ."

"What about the toilet handles that are all mangled from Toby chewing them? And we have to remember to tell her about his bathroom fetish."

Another example came to mind. "Remember, Christopher, the very first big Toby incident? How we couldn't even get in the garage entrance because he'd piled so much crap in front of the door?" The memories came more and more quickly. "We can't forget about the time he was at the dog sitters, when we were in Halifax at the conference, and he took their whole screen door out when he raced out after a squirrel. Oh, and there was the time you swore that someone must have broken into the house because the only thing disturbed was the very top bookshelf, and everything else was perfect. That was weird. I'm adding that. . . . Honey, what's wrong?"

Christopher's smile was tight. "Jeez, Char, you talk about the things he's done as if they're cute and funny. Why do you always have to try and make light of this or find the positive in everything? You're grinning away to yourself. It's not cute. It's not funny. It's my life, and it's pretty annoying."

"You're right. You're right. These incidents weren't funny at the time, but talking about them now . . . well, some of them are pretty amusing."

"Really?"

I didn't enjoy Christopher when he acted like this, just as he probably didn't care for me when I was frustrated. I hadn't meant to offend him. Even though I had worked for many years as a mediator helping others resolve conflict, I didn't like it much when the tables were turned, and the conflict was my own.

Sometimes silence can be so loud. Even Toby, still locked in the bathroom, had fallen quiet. The ticking of the clock above the kitchen table was the loudest sound in the house. Finally, Christopher pushed his chair back and stood.

"I think you can handle the list by yourself. I'm going to bed."

My chin in my hands, I looked up at him. We both believed in working through disagreements until a solution was found, and in the past, I would never let him walk off and go to bed in the middle of a fight. But I knew there was no solution in this case. It was us against Toby, or us and Toby against separation anxiety. I didn't know what it was. I couldn't wait for the dog behaviorist to arrive.

After Chris went upstairs, I walked to the bathroom and opened the door. "Come on, Toby. Time for bed." Instead of going into his kennel, Toby followed me upstairs and went to sleep on the floor on Chris's side of the bed.

When our doorbell rang the next day, Toby went

berserk, barking and racing down the stairs so fast he missed the last five steps entirely.

"Toby!" I said. "Enough! *Ssshhh.* Stop it! Get in the garage!"

I wondered if our guest had heard all that from the front porch. Well, if so, she was forewarned: scolding Toby had absolutely no positive effect. In fact, it seemed that Toby interpreted the phrase "bad boy" as "go get your favorite toy and roll around in ecstasy." He seemed to believe that a Kong—a hollow rubber chew toy filled with dog treats with a rope on it—or a Frisbee, or a ball were the solutions to any problem. *Char and Chris are mad at me? Here's a ball! If I offer to play with them, all will be forgiven!*

When I finally opened the front door, I was surprised to see a thin, gentle-looking woman standing there. She did not match my picture of a dog trainer—which I guess maybe was a stern-looking, masterful type, like a lion tamer. A strong wind practically blew Maggie into the house. Laughing, she straightened her denim jacket and put her hair back in order. When Toby's barking stopped, I opened the garage and he bounded in, barking his head off and dancing around Maggie and me in the spacious front hall.

"Toby!" I cried. "Toby, sit! Sorry, Maggie, just a minute. *Toby!*" I grabbed his collar and tried to keep him and his slobber off Maggie's pants. He finally sat down—but a moment later was back on his feet, whining in excitement and nudging Maggie's leg.

Maggie made a shushing noise. Then, "Toby, sit!"

Toby dropped like a stone onto his haunches. I almost did, too. I couldn't quite believe such a firm voice had come from such a diminutive person.

Maggie stood and stretched one arm at a downward angle, finger pointing at the floor, a look of gentle determination on her face. Panting, Toby gazed up at her, utterly spellbound.

"Thank you," I said. "Well, that's great. Umm . . . I'm Charmaine, and I guess you've met Toby."

"Yes." She smiled.

"And here comes my husband, Chris," I said, as he walked in, hand outstretched. "Should we give you a quick tour around Toby's world—his surroundings?"

"That would be great, thanks."

Maggie eased her way around Toby and me, then walked into the main part of the house. Toby rose to follow. Without turning, she shot an arm toward him, finger pointed. "Sit!" She flipped the same hand palm up. "Stay." Then, without missing a beat, she said, "You have a lovely home, Charmaine."

Toby sat waiting, his tail wagging and his big, pink tongue hanging out the side of his mouth.

"Thank you . . ." I said, inching after her, hardly daring to breathe as I passed Toby—who, unbelievably, still sat staring after her. Christopher joined me and Maggie as we moved into the kitchen.

"Who is this woman?" he whispered from the corner of his mouth, keeping his gaze on Toby. "Can we put her on retainer for life? Or maybe let her keep Toby, and we just have visitation rights?"

As Maggie toured the house with us, I recited the low points of Toby's behavioral history.

Toby started whining. I said, "I think he's getting a little antsy."

"He's fine. Let's talk about why I'm here."

"Yes, exactly," Chris said.

We returned to the kitchen, and I positioned myself in front of the hall so Toby could see me. I took a deep breath. "We adopted this dog nine months ago. We've found him to be a challenge, and our vet recommended talking to you. Just to see if there's something that can be done." Another whine, this one drawn out and heartbreaking. "He has a condition that he might really need to be on medication for, so your techniques may not work. But we thought it was worth a shot." The whole time I spoke, Chris stood beside me nodded.

"Oh, I think I might have some suggestions that will work," Maggie said. "They almost always work. Toby, come."

Toby sprinted into the kitchen and came skidding to a stop a few feet past Maggie.

"It's good you're doing this," she said to us as Toby wriggled with excitement. "Not just for yourselves, but for Toby, too. The most important thing is Toby's safety, and that knife block incident is worrisome."

"It scared us," I said. "We've already taken steps to increase Toby's safety. Christopher comes home for lunch now, reducing the time Toby's alone each day, and we've dog-proofed the house as best we can. The knife block is in the cupboard, we took all the breakable stuff off the counter, and we try extra hard to close all the doors when we leave."

"Those are all good," she said. "What else?"

"Well, we relocated our water cooler into my office, which is always locked when we aren't home."

Chris pulled out a chair. "In fact, we've practically put away everything we ever wanted to live with," he said. "When is enough, enough?"

"That's one of the things we have to figure out." Maggie made herself comfortable. "I'm here to observe, so pretend I'm not here. Just go about your lives like normal so I can get an idea of what Toby's really like."

Easier said than done. Normally, Christopher would be gone to work by now, and I'd be busy in my office with Toby sleeping beside me. Or I might be gone at a conference, which would mean Toby would be home alone. None of these scenarios were easily replicable. I suddenly knew how the people on reality television feel.

So Chris and I simply settled ourselves at the kitchen table. Toby paced between us, looking for attention. When he didn't find it, he headed into the living room, then came back into the kitchen.

After this went on for a while, I told Maggie Toby often did this, wandering around aimlessly between Chris and me. "He seems to be going between the two of you to make sure you're okay," Maggie said. "He walks over to you, Charmaine, checks that you're fine, then moves to Chris, then back again. He really seems to be focused on making sure everyone in the house is doing all right. Like that's his job."

"But why doesn't he calm down when he sees we're fine?" Chris said.

"Just because you're fine one moment doesn't mean you'll be fine the next."

Chris sighed in vexation. "None of this answers the big question: why does Toby trash our house when we're gone?"

I waited anxiously for the answer. If Maggie couldn't

help us with that problem, nothing else mattered. Every time we closed the door of the house behind us, we were filled with trepidation, not knowing what we'd find when we came home. I couldn't even admit to just how far this fear had pushed me.

In my work as a professional business speaker and facilitator, I helped audiences understand the importance of having a positive mindset and setting positive intentions to others. So whenever I left, I found myself trying to send Toby affirmative mental messages: *Have a wonderful day, Toby. You are confident, secure, and well behaved. You handle being alone successfully. You feel no need to turn the house inside-out. . . .*

I used affirmations for Chris and me, too. *We will return to an intact home. Everything will be in its place. We will enjoy the feeling of happiness as Toby proudly shows us he is capable of being a good dog in our absence. Our shoes will be in the closet, the furniture will be where we left it, and there will be no broken toilet tank lids.*

Maggie was watching Toby pausing at his food bowl to snap up some kibble as he wandered back and forth. "Does he always do that?"

"Yes, that's his M.O.," I said, looking nervously at Christopher. Was Toby's eating style a problem, too?

"It's aimless," said Maggie. "A symptom of anxiety. He isn't comfortable staying put and enjoying his meal. He isn't sure that focusing on his dinner is all he has to do."

"What else could he have to do?" Chris said. "He's a dog."

"Oh, you'd be surprised."

Christopher raised his eyebrows at me, an expression as

revealing as one of Toby's: *Is she kidding?* "So . . ." he asked, "How does one get to be an animal behaviorist?"

"If you're wondering about my training and experience," Maggie replied with a smile, "I have an extensive background training dogs, as well as teaching obedience classes to owners and their pets."

"I didn't mean—"

"No, it's a perfectly legitimate question." Maggie described the details of her professional experience, and within a few sentences, Chris was nodding. Clearly we were in good hands.

"Regarding the way Toby damages your house," Maggie said, "this is a big place; it gives Toby too much to worry about. I suggest you kennel him when you're gone, or section off a part of the house to keep him in. It would have to be down here because of the open design of your home."

"There's a kennel in the basement," Christopher said.

"Perfect. Keep him in it when you go out. And keep the basement dark, so it will feel like a den for him. Most likely he'll just settle in and go to sleep."

She suggested we give Toby a special stuffed animal to care for while we were away, a toy he got only when we were leaving, and put away the minute we got home. She also suggested that we provide Toby with opportunities to work.

"Work?" I said.

"When you take him out to play, structure some of the activities as work or training. Try to differentiate his 'play' time and his 'training or work' time. Say, 'Let's go work, Toby,' so he knows he's doing something different from the usual game of catch. You might also want to use a different leash or collar for the two activities, so he associates one leash with play and the other with training. Also, do you run him or exercise him before you leave to go somewhere? It would suppress his nervous energy and reduce his boredom, which would likely improve his behavior."

"We try to do that," Christopher said, "but we could probably do more."

"Maggie," I said, "we've noticed that Toby has issues with certain noises. He's afraid of the printer, the fax machine, the washing machine buzzer, the garbage truck, and the mixer."

"And the tire compressor," Chris added.

"The ringing of the doorbell always inspires a barking fit," I said. "It was a relief when the batteries on it died; we never replaced them. Thunderstorms are another story; they really seem to inspire his 'bad boy' side. He senses storms coming long before they get here and starts pacing; then starts taking restless walks to the bathroom, and finally closes himself in there. When we rescue him, he goes right back to pacing and checking on everyone in the house. If we're not here when the storm breaks, he shoves furniture around like he's trying to escape the noise."

"And if you are home?"

"Then he gallops in and jumps into either my or Chris's lap—all ninety pounds of him. He's no lap dog."

Maggie nodded. "A lot of dogs fear thunder and lightning; they're very aware of weather changes. Some dogs hide and cower, and others behave like Toby. How do you two respond when Toby acts fearful?"

I had to think on that. What *did* we do? "Well, typically I try to reassure him. I pet him and say something like 'It's okay, Toby. Everything's fine.'"

"Sometimes, the way in which people reassure dogs creates an adverse effect; it actually *escalates* the anxiety. Instead of trying to soothe him, divert his attention away from the noise. Tell him to go get his ball or that Kong toy he loves so much. If he's focused on something besides the noise, he won't be able to react to it."

I felt as if a concrete block had just floated off my shoulders. "It's important to be consistent," she said, "and not make a big deal of these noises, or of Toby's anxious response to them. For example, when I arrived, I heard Toby's reaction from outside, and then you shouting at him, Charmaine. But when Toby's barking, he's not listening to you as a leader. So when the doorbell rings, direct Toby to sit and stay. If he moves, bring him back and repeat the command. He can come to the front door when you direct him to, but not whenever he chooses."

I glanced at Chris. Now his expression said, *She's good.*

But she wasn't finished yet. "Do you have another dog besides Toby?"

Chris let out a bray of laughter.

"No," I said, giving him a look. "Just Toby. Why?"

"He's unsure of his role in your family, and that's causing him a great deal of anxiety."

I knew what Christopher was going to say before the words left his mouth: "His *role?* He's a dog. His role is to be a dog. Bark, pee, go for walks. What are you talking about?"

I didn't share my husband's cynicism. I knew Maggie was on to something. For any intelligent being, having a role, a purpose in life, is critical. I saw the truth of this every day in my work. Some people lived with passion and purpose, while others were searching for a purpose to guide their lives. There was a big difference between the two groups.

Maggie faced Christopher with a warm smile. "Imagine if you had nothing to do all day, every day. Or what if you sensed that nothing you did mattered—to anyone? What if you just aimlessly wandered around while everyone around you came and went doing important things? Or you felt like you had to take care of this big house by yourself while everyone else was gone? How would you respond?"

"I'd be listless," I said, my eyes starting to well over. I understood what Maggie was saying. Toby didn't feel like part of our family. He was struggling to know whose dog he was, to whom he should be loyal. My heart ached for the poor, confused animal.

But Christopher's jaw was set. "No offense, Maggie, but how we'd respond isn't the point. We're not dogs. Toby's a dog. It's how he responds that matters. And how he responds is . . . badly."

This time I had to back up my husband. "We do give Toby the responsibility of watching the house. We say 'Guard the house' every time we leave, just like with did with our first dog. It worked with Dooks, but it doesn't seem to matter to Toby."

"'Watch the house' is a passive command—more like a suggestion. Toby is a retriever, a working dog. Working dogs do best when they have *jobs*. Not just vague directions— active, specific tasks to accomplish." She scratched Toby under the chin. "This is actually a very good dog. He's gentle, smart, well trained, people oriented, and responsive. Even while he's just lying here on the floor, he's alert to our conversation. He looks up when he hears familiar words. He's constantly focused on checking on you both, making sure you're okay. But again, he needs a *real* job."

I exchanged a glance with Chris. "Um . . . we think Toby's problems are in part due to stress. We think he got separation anxiety from missing his previous owners. Wouldn't a job just cause more stress and more problems?"

"Char, he's not going back to his previous owners, so there's no point in worrying about that. And the stress isn't going away on its own. Think about it—without something to do, don't you think even you might feel like tearing the closet apart from time to time?"

"I suppose that makes sense. It would burn up some of his energy, anyway," I said.

"Okay . . ." Chris said. "So what sort of job is available for the four-legged?"

"I think Toby would make a good pet-assisted therapy dog. He has the right temperament for it."

She explained that pet-assisted therapy was a common form of therapy used to help individuals and groups deal with a variety of issues. "People get so many benefits from physical contact with animals. It can improve physical skills, mental capacity, and the ability to learn."

"I kind of picture those animals as being calm and docile," said Christopher. "Toby would be leaping all over his patients."

"Well, we won't sign him up today. I suggest obedience classes as a first step. That will give him the opportunity to sharpen his people skills while we prepare him for pet-assisted therapy. And it will help you sharpen your skills in helping Toby learn boundaries, too."

We signed up for the next round of classes.

By now, Toby was on his feet again, wagging his tail and nudging us with his big snout: *Yes yes yes!* Once again he seemed to understand the spoken word, or at least the intent behind the words.

"He looks excited," I said, and gave him a cuddle. "Looks like you're getting a job, buddy!"

"Wow, I wish I could get that excited about working," Chris dryly. Then, "How much will he be making? He owes me $1,314.67 for toilet tank lids—not including my costs for installation."

Twelve

Boot Camp

We put Maggie's suggestions into practice the moment she left, beginning by sectioning off the basement to provide Toby with less house to worry about—or have access to—in our absence.

"I bet the Home Depot guys were surprised when you left with a baby gate instead of a toilet tank lid," I teased Chris. "There might be some interesting rumors flying around there about us."

Installation complete, Christopher closed the gate and firmly told Toby to "Stay and guard the house." Then we left for a while. Our plan was to increase the length of our absences from a few minutes to a few hours to allow Toby to adjust to his new circumstances.

After about five minutes, we returned, opened the front

door . . . and were greeted by a smiling Toby, tail wagging and pink tongue flopping out of the side of his mouth. *Ta da!*

"Well, this worked great," Christopher said sarcastically, as he went down to check out the gate. It looked as if Toby had jumped over it, knocking it down in the process. Chris shook his head. "This won't work; the staircase is designed in a way that won't let us get a tight fit with the gate unless we do some major construction. And we know we can't close him up in a room; we'll come home to a complete disaster."

Of course, we were irritated at the wasted forty dollars and the time it had taken to put the gate up. Toby, on the other hand, seemed very pleased with his accomplishment—an admirable skill if you're a prisoner on a penal island in the Mediterranean, but not in a nice home in Sherwood Park.

Still, I had to bend down and scratch under his chin. "You're big on solving problems, aren't you, my little monster?" Toby flopped on the floor so I could get to his belly. "So why don't you solve this problem: what should Char and Chris do about Toby?"

A blissed-out Toby gave no response.

Well, if we couldn't section off a piece of the house, we'd try the kennel approach. It sounded like a good plan: his big plastic kennel had always been a safe haven for him, and he loved to sleep in it. He never seemed to mind being closed in the kennel for an hour or so.

Initially, our new strategy seemed to do the trick; I'd come home from work to Toby napping happily in his kennel. But on garbage day, I returned just in time to find him chewing his way out of the enclosure. I immediately released him, worried that he'd cut his gums or damage his teeth on the hard plastic. He trembled constantly and wouldn't leave my side for hours.

"I don't know if this is going to work, Christopher," I said when my husband got home.

"It has to. What are our options?"

He was right; we had none. A few days later, we coaxed Toby back into the kennel the same way as before, at first leaving him for several minutes at a time, praising him for being a good boy, and eventually extending the time and going out of the house entirely. Surprisingly, he adjusted to the kennel again and seemed okay as long as we didn't leave him for too long.

Encouraged, we tried some of Maggie's other suggestions. We turned a stuffed brown bear into Toby's "Take care of this while we're gone" toy, and he nurtured that bear like his own puppy. However, the success of this tactic depended entirely on our consistency in applying it (a great lesson in life) and other less controllable factors, like thunderstorms, garbage trucks, the doorbell ringing, or the house alarm accidentally going off.

Toby's Boot Camp, designed to whip him into shape, featured more exercise, more socialization, and more focused activities. We played hide-and-seek, visited busy areas of town, and went on play dates with his neighborhood friends. Chris practiced obedience commands with him every night. We implemented Maggie's advice on how to handle Toby when someone came to the door, and it worked beautifully. We also dealt with his barking the way Maggie had taught us.

The goal was to help Toby identify Christopher and me as his pack leaders, so he could better manage his anxiety and thus his behavior. Slowly, we saw progress. Toby seemed more confident and was less of a shadow. Almost all his misbehavior occurred when he was home alone.

But that was bad enough. Closet emptying was a weekly occurrence, and we could find no pattern to explain why. Twice more, Christopher had to repair the boot racks and twice more, Toby took them out again. After one closet repair, Chris removed some of the coats and shoes we didn't wear that often and placed them in the closet in the garage. Smart man; there would be less to tidy up next time.

That afternoon we called Maggie, explained the continued closet emptying, and asked what it meant.

"Dogs may do that when they're anxious. It may be that he's hiding in there to feel safe, like in a den. He might stop that when he realizes your new routines are good and consistent. Did you have any luck finding him a job?"

"We're researching what programs are available. We'll keep you posted."

She suggested that in the meantime, we try the kennel again. I made a mental note to give her a call in a couple of weeks to let her know how Toby was doing and the status on the job search.

One afternoon, I left briefly to pick up my niece, who was visiting from Ontario before coming to live with us to attend college in the fall. When we got back to the house, we went straight to see Toby, but he wasn't there. The door of the kennel hung open.

"I didn't just double-check that lock, Ashley," I said, "I *triple*-checked it. How in the heck did he get out? Toby!"

He slunk into view.

"Toby! What am I going to find when I look in the hall-way?"

Ashley raised her eyebrows. "How bad can it be, Auntie Char?"

It was bad. He'd emptied the closet yet again, tearing coats from hangers and scattering shoes from one end of the house to the other. But apparently, that was not enough. The basement shelves had been cleared, two of the dining room chairs lay on their sides, and one had been pushed into the living room where a big plant had also been tipped over. He'd emptied the pot and chewed off half its side; little pieces of beige and green plastic lay everywhere. Downstairs, we found remnants of the bedding from his kennel everywhere.

We also found Toby's little brown stuffed bear, wet from being groomed with Toby's tongue.

Ashley looked stunned. "Wow, Auntie, I thought you were exaggerating when you said Toby was a bit like a hurricane."

"If he keeps this up, I'm going to have to crate him for the rest of his life." I purposely chose the word "crate" because Toby didn't know it. Chris and I had always used the word "kennel" around him.

Ashley bent to hug Toby. "Oh, he'll learn. Won't you, Toby? You're a good boy. Tell Auntie Char you're a good boy." Then she deepened her voice, speaking for Toby. "I'm sorry, Mom, I just missed you. Don't stuff me in a crate for the rest of my life."

An hour later, I put Toby in his kennel in the basement again so Ashley and I could make a quick trip to the store. When we returned fifteen minutes later, Toby had chewed the handles off the kennel so the door could no longer be secured. I found him in the living room lying on his mat, his stuffed bear under his head, his face the picture of innocence.

I turned to Ashley. "I think that dog reads the dictionary when we're not looking."

Toby just grinned.

Hidden Treasures

In spite of the ongoing mayhem, Toby was beginning to grow on Christopher. I was already in love with Toby, of course, and had been since I'd met him. But it was touching to see Toby and Chris bonding more. Watching Chris cuddle with Toby while he watched TV or read a book was a sign that everything might just be okay after all.

Besides, it was difficult to stay angry with Toby. How could we not love being greeted with such unconditional love, even when we'd only been in the next room? He knew our routines well and would wait excitedly at the window to see Chris driving home from work; he rushed to the door as soon as he heard me getting my coat for our afternoon walk. He loved nothing better than to cozy up with Chris and me to watch a movie and would park himself on the floor between our feet, undoubtedly wishing he could finagle his way onto the couch.

There were many days when I wondered why I had ever complained about Toby.

There were other days when I wondered why I had ever *not* complained about Toby.

And then there was the day disaster turned to something miraculous.

One evening, after returning from the gym, Chris and I were greeted at the door by a very happy-looking Toby. A quick look around told us everything was intact. I was delighted. I had worked hard to set Toby up for success for the short time he'd be home alone—throwing the ball to him outside to burn off some energy and closing all doors prior to our departure. It was nice to see that the effort had paid off.

"Good boy, Toby," I said as we checked the kitchen and living room. No problems. But as I opened the fridge to get his dinner, something caught my eye. At the top of the stairs, the bedroom door was open. Uh-oh. As I climbed the steps, Toby looked a bit sheepish and did not follow me. That was a sure sign that a bad-boy incident had occurred.

I looked into the bedroom. The five-foot-tall standing mirror lay on its side, although thankfully the glass had not broken. My jewelry had been strewn across the floor.

I heard Chris stop breathing behind me. "Well," I said, "at least he didn't knock over the plants. That would have been a terrible mess on the carpet."

Chris just shook his head and headed for the shower.

A moment later, Toby peeked in the bedroom door. "Toby!" I said. "How could you? We were only gone a little while. Now Christopher is mad at you again, and I'm going to have to clean up this mess." I was exhausted and near tears. Who needed a dog that couldn't be left alone for a measly hour and a half?

Then, as I started picking up the jewelry, I realized that they weren't the valuables from my everyday jewelry box. These items came from my keepsake box, which had apparently been behind the mirror Toby had knocked over. I hadn't thought about that box in years. In fact, I didn't even recall putting the keepsake box back there; I would have sworn it was high on a shelf in my clothes closet.

As I picked each piece of jewelry off the carpet, my annoyance slowly shifted into pleasure. I was flooded with wonderful memories of the person who'd given the piece to me and recalled what my life had been like when I received it. Here was the beautiful pin given to me by my Aunt Dorothy when I was ten or eleven. "Look at this, Toby!" I said. "I felt so grown up when I got this. I remember wearing it to school with such pride."

Next I found something more precious than a jewel: my first birthday candle. That had been around for a while! Here were coins from England, given to me by my great-grandfather when I was a little girl who found them as captivating as the gold and jewels in storybooks. I could almost hear my great granddad calling a greeting in his British accent: "Aidy Aie." I used to call him my Aidy Aie Grandad because of this greeting.

I scooped up a pin that had once adorned my Highland dancing kilt. I'd been so proud of that kilt! My best friend, Rose Anne, and I had taken classes together. How many performances had I given my family in the living room?

And at university, in the computer lab after cramming for exams, I had once shown my classmates my personal rendition of the sword dance and a Celtic river dance.

Then there were the singing performances of "Lonely Little Robin" my two sisters and I would give our grandparents in the living room. Even as adults, we serenaded them with this song. When my granddad died, I sang it in my head as I said good-bye to him.

One by one, I picked up the little charms for a charm bracelet that our neighbors and family members had given me. And here was the gold stud earring from when I got my ears pierced as a young teenager; I felt so mature that day. Tucked almost under the bed was a note on a piece of faded cardboard attached to a ring from a bubblegum machine. It was from my sister Melanie, written when she was about nine years old. In her big, childlike hand, it said, "Charmaine loves Chris." Of course, when she gave me this gift, she also sang "Charmaine and Chris, sitting in a tree. K-I-S-S-I-N-G."

A movie of my life was running in my mind . . . and in my heart.

As though he knew I was about to speak to him, Toby ran over to me. I hugged him. "I'd completely forgotten about all these things, Toby."

A glint of silver under the dresser caught my eye: a one-dollar coin from 1975. My grandmother, my mom's mother, had sent it to me with a note: "A keepsake for good luck and good fortune." I held it up to Toby. "My lucky dollar! Boy, I could have used this over the years." I rubbed and kissed it. "Toby, I just wished for you to be a good dog from this day forward."

I had lost all sense of time. Chris found me sitting on the floor, and I held up the dollar. "When I was a little girl, I spent hours going through my grandma's keepsake drawer, making her tell and retell the stories attached to each piece. These things have been hidden away. I'd almost forgotten their stories. Toby scattered them everywhere, naturally. But what a wonderful treat!"

Christopher picked up a gold necklace covered with multicolored gemstones. "What's the story with this one?"

It was my other grandmother's necklace. I took it from Chris, savoring it while waiting for the lump in my throat to soften. The rubies and other gems glittered in the light from the window. "My father bought this for his mother when he was a young man. Grandma always wore it with pride. I can still picture her at Christmas, alive with excitement at having her whole family around. The necklace was as important a tradition as the tree. After dinner, my dad's family would pick up their various instruments—Grandma played several—and they'd sing together. I would sit on the staircase, letting the music of my family wash over me and fill my heart. Chris, I can see it so clearly, it's like I could reach out and touch them. It makes me ache to think about it, but in a good way. What I wouldn't give to be back on that staircase one more time. I miss mom and dad, and my sisters."

In a soft voice, Chris said, "Amazing, isn't it, that all these years together, we still have things to share, pieces of our pasts to share. What a lovely knowing."

"Yes," I said, "For a precious moment, I was back in my parents' house, the smell of roast turkey mingling with the scent of the Christmas tree and my uncle's tobacco, feeling that comforting sense of safety, that all-pervasive love, that lucky children feel when surrounded by family. A priceless moment!"

Toby always knew when my tears were falling. He came to my side and started licking my face, trying to make it better. I laughed. "It's okay, Toby. These are good tears. This was a good thing. Thanks for the mess! And the memories."

Ready to transform a heartfelt moment into a fun one, Toby began doing what Chris and I referred to as his Happy Dance—sitting down, eyes bright and wide, mouth open, tongue hanging to one side as he wagged his tail at a speed that caused his entire body to vibrate. To accompany the dance, he made an unusual "awwwww" sound that always made us laugh.

The happy dance was part of Toby's morning routine, and we adored it. He wouldn't stop until he received a snuggle. It was like he was making a trade: a good laugh for a little affection.

Christopher smiled at me, and I hugged our crazy dog. "You goof. It's okay; no one's mad at you anymore. What you did wasn't so terrible. In fact, you did me a favor. I needed to be reminded of my own reminders, and I'm going to put my keepsakes where I can see them more often."

Chris said, "He's lucky he's so easy to forgive."

"I was just thinking that myself. I'm glad you feel the same way. We get so upset with him, but there's really nothing to do but accept his behavior." Toby shoved his nose in my ear. "Get out. You know, Christopher, if I were half as willing to accept my own shortcomings and failures as I am to accept Toby's, I'd be an extraordinarily happy woman."

Christopher closed the lid on my keepsake box. "I guess we're all more accepting of others' mistakes. Look at how often I have to forgive you."

I laughed. "Me? Please. I'm perfect. Come on, you messy animal," I said to Toby. "Let's get you your dinner." His crime forgiven and forgotten, Toby happily followed me downstairs.

Fourteen

Teacher's Pet

We entered our second round of obedience classes with Maggie. Toby had done incredibly well in the first round. He knew all the commands, but what the program had done most was help him build confidence, provide additional socialization with other dogs, and allow Toby to see Chris and me as the leaders of our pack. Of course, there was a down side, as usual—the drive to Maggie's house for obedience class every Monday night was a noisy one, with Toby's barking reaching a near-deafening level as we made the turn onto Maggie's street.

After a quick stroll around the yard to let Toby do his business, we opened Maggie's door. Toby always had to go in first, shoving his way between us and stepping into the room with an air of importance and a joyful bark. He cast his gaze around the room, perhaps counting the number of dogs—usually about six, along with their owners—then gave a series of barks that seemed to serve as individual greetings.

Toby was in his glory in Maggie's classes. He tried to be first at everything, and loved it when he was chosen to model the next activity.

But his penchant for being first and best didn't always work for him. "Now that everyone understands the technique for getting your dog to go through the tunnel," Maggie said, "let's all give it a try."

As usual, Toby shoved his way to the front of the line.

"Does anyone want to go first?" Maggie said, pretending to look around the room. "Anyone? Anyone?" Finally she looked down at Toby's wriggling form. "Oh, Toby. How unlike you. All right. Go to it, then."

Navigating the tunnel looked like a fairly easy task, and I was confident Toby could do it. I led him toward the tunnel while encouraging him the way Maggie had demonstrated. But at the last second, apparently eager to accomplish the goal of reaching the finish line first, Toby made the decision to skip the tunnel altogether, and ran beside it. What a time-saver. He sat down at the tunnel exit and barked at Maggie to reward him with a treat.

Maggie crossed her arms and looked down at him. "Oh no. Back you go."

"Stay," I said as we prepared to try again. "Okay, Toby, through the tunnel. Go, go, go!" Toby took off toward the tunnel—and once again ran beside it. He reached the end and barked.

Hands on her hips, Maggie shook her head.

On the third try, Toby entered the tunnel, but turned around midway and came out the way he'd gone in, looking happy. Hmm. Maybe my very, very smart dog wasn't so smart after all.

But with Maggie's help, Toby caught on the fourth time around, erupting from the correct end of the tunnel to cheers from the class. He beamed and proudly accepted his treat from Maggie. Although it had taken him a while to pick up the tunnel routine, he never forgot it; in fact, it became his favorite activity at obedience class. As he waited in line for his turn, he would squirm with excitement, looking for all the world like a little kid at Christmas.

One evening, Maggie directed all the dogs to lie down side by side. "Can I get the owners to tell the dogs to stay and then leave the room, please?" she said. Toby lay in a row with two boxers, a Shih Tzu, an Airedale terrier, and a Weimaraner. I felt my gut tighten. "This should be interesting," I whispered to Chris.

"Stay, Toby," said Christopher, and we walked out of the room with the other owners, leaving Maggie and the dogs. Glancing back as I walked out, I noticed Toby watching us. "He's not going to last two seconds," I said to Chris.

While we were in the other room, I could hear movement and Maggie's voice, no doubt commanding Toby to get back in line. I closed my eyes and leaned against the wall.

"Your dog is very . . . spirited." A woman's rather high-pitched voice, right in my ear. I opened my eyes and smiled at the Weimaraner's owner.

"Yes. He is." I tried to think of something nice to say

about her dog, a large, docile animal with a shy personality. "Yours is very well mannered."

"Thank you. I've had a lot of dogs. It's all in how you handle them from day one."

I nodded and began to move toward Christopher, but she wasn't giving up so easily. "Huggie is going to be a pet-assisted therapy dog when she finishes here."

"Oh? So is Toby!"

Her expression could have soured milk. "I wouldn't get my hopes up about that dog, dear. Only the very best animals, the best behaved, are selected to help with therapy programs." She chuckled. "I can just see Toby racing through the hospital corridors dragging some poor child in a wheelchair or pulling someone's oxygen tank behind him."

I glanced at Chris, who was reading a quote on the calendar on the wall. The quote had something to do with dogs leaving paw prints on our hearts. Suddenly he turned to the woman. "Well, I know Toby is a bit energetic, but it was Maggie's suggestion he be a therapy dog. Toby is great with people; he'll make a difference in people's lives."

What was this? Chris defending Toby? I felt strengthened knowing that even though Chris didn't always seem to be listening, he was.

The woman glanced at Chris then back at me with pity in her eyes. "Yes. I'm sure."

The door opened, and Maggie motioned us back in. To my amazement, there was Toby lying quietly in the same position as when we had left. Smiling, Chris and I walked toward him, congratulating him all the way. Tail wagging, eyes bright, tongue hanging out, Toby stayed in place and barked once. *Thanks.*

"Toby was the best of the bunch," said Maggie. "He didn't move, was very obedient, and wasn't distracted by the other dogs."

My heart swelled with pride. In spite of myself, I glanced at Huggie's owner. She seemed to be avoiding my eyes. I resisted the urge to say, "I told you so."

My dear husband was less restrained. "Told you so," he chirped, as he scratched Toby's head. Only we could hear him, but we felt so much better. It was good to believe in Toby, to finally have some hope.

After class, I approached Maggie and asked about Toby's potential as a pet-assisted therapy dog. She didn't even glance up. "He's perfect. You should get going on that."

"He doesn't exactly seem perfect," I said. "He's still so rambunctious. Don't you have to be gentle and well behaved to be involved with therapy?"

Maggie smiled. "Toby is gentle. He doesn't need to be perfect, Charmaine. I've never seen him be aggressive or come across too strong. He's highly intuitive, and he behaves appropriately given a particular situation. Trust me; he's going to be excellent in his job." She simultaneously patted my arm and Toby's head. "And remember, Toby *needs* to do this. He needs a purpose in life, and if you don't find him one, you may never get him to stop destroying your house."

It seemed to be true. The boot-camp approach and weekly obedience classes seemed to be leading to some positive behavior changes in Toby and a lot less stress for us. He still emptied the closet and bookshelves fairly regularly, but the incidents were less frequent, and the extent of the destruction was down.

Fifteen

Failure with Honor

With Maggie's encouragement, we identified several pet-assisted therapy programs. I attended an orientation meeting with a local pet-therapy association to inquire about Toby being a volunteer visitor in a hospital or with children. It had been years since I had worked with children, and I was excited about the possibility of volunteering with them. Toby's energy would be a good match for kids—I certainly couldn't see him succeeding in a senior facility or geriatric unit.

After what felt like a long wait, our application for the test was finally processed and a test date set. Christopher and I had been practicing the exercises and training commands with Toby; we were confident that he would do well.

On the way to the test building, Toby was full of excitement, bouncing around in the back seat, poking his nose into the front. Not that he knew where we were going, nor cared. He was in a car and with us, and that was all that mattered.

Still, his excitement grew as we walked toward the building. "Toby, wait," I said. "Slow." He was pulling hard on his leash, charging toward the door and the sound of other dogs and people.

But when we opened the door, Toby became a little unnerved. A large group of people and dogs crowded a room the size of a double garage. Christopher, skilled at introducing Toby to new environments, made a point of displaying confidence and walked Toby around the room. Toby started barking, one of his ways of coping as he becomes familiar with new surroundings. He settled just in time for the tests to begin.

The tests were designed to check an animal's ability to handle situations it would encounter as a pet-therapy animal. Toby walked into a crowd, visited with a person in a wheelchair, and had his foot pinched and tail pulled. Cookie sheets were tossed in front of him, something that could have frightened him, but he remained calm. One exercise required Toby to go through a door with dogs on the other side and several people calling his name and petting him as he moved through the doorway. This was bliss for Toby. Dogs, people, and petting all at once. Could life get better?

"He did great," said Christopher after Toby finished the nine or ten different tests. We praised and cuddled Toby, and the look on his face was one of pure joy, big pink tongue flopping to the side of his mouth, tail wagging a hundred miles an hour.

Then the instructor came to deliver the results. "Toby did very well with the tests, but we can't pass him because of his barking." She explained, at great length, that barking was not conducive to a pet-therapy dog and that most environments and facilities would not accept him because of it.

As we left, Christopher put his arm around me, sensing that I, more than Toby, needed reassurance. We'd been working on the antibarking suggestions Maggie gave us in class, trying to catch Toby before he barked, using the command "leave it" and saying "Shhh!" with the hand signal—and Toby had made big improvements.

"This breaks my heart, Chris," I said. "Toby gave his best. I was so proud of him. Now what? Will we ever find him a job?"

Christopher gave me a squeeze. I thought of how, before, I had compared Toby to a teenager. Now he was like a young man, becoming independent—and he'd just had his first failure.

On this occasion, Toby fortunately seemed oblivious to what had happened. All he knew was that he had had a ton of fun and made us proud. He settled happily in the back seat, basking in the feeling of a job well done. I wished I could do the same. After all, he had done a good job. But I was worried about what the future would look like if we were unable to find a long-term job, a purpose, for Toby.

Sixteen

Get a Job

Toby spent the next two months in his usual way: being well behaved much of the time, and the rest of the time emptying closets, trapping himself in the bathroom, and engaging in numerous other behaviors that kept Christopher and me busy. We were learning that we needed to take more responsibility for reducing the opportunities that Toby had to wreak havoc, so we became more diligent about closing all doors (especially the bathroom) when we left to go out. Meanwhile, we continued to search for a job for him, but there didn't seem to be many options.

"Perhaps," I said, "we should hire him out as a farmhand to round up sheep or cattle."

Chris scoffed. "I think he'd really shine working with a demolition crew."

Even so, Toby's confidence was slowly improving. We noticed that he was more likely to walk a little further ahead (a meter or two) of us, without constantly looking behind to check that we were still there. He continued to be extremely obedient in our presence, following all basic commands, but he was also able to sit with a treat on the floor in front of him for two to three minutes and not taking the treat until directed to do so. *His* patience improved—and so did ours!

We finally came across information on a program that sounded perfect for Toby: the Chimo Animal Assisted Therapy Project. This organization certifies not only dogs but cats, rabbits, birds, and mini-horses as therapy animals to work with people suffering from a range of mental health issues in hospitals, group homes, and schools. The Project looks for animals that show an obvious love for people, approach new situations with confidence, are obedient and friendly, and are happiest when they are the center of attention.

I continued reading, excited to learn more about this—after all, Toby and I would be volunteering together. The research I immersed myself in described Animal Assisted Therapy (AAT) as a goal-directed intervention or program whereby an animal is an integral part of the treatment process or therapeutic program. Therapists who use AAT help clients make changes with the assistance of the animals. Chimo's programs and the facilities where they place animals help people with diverse medical and mental health issues.

Given my background in counseling and mediation, I found this intriguing.

"Chris. Check this out. It's amazing the role animals can play in the treatment of people. Animals in this program help with stress reduction, increase peoples' ability to bond and have healthy relationships, build confidence, provide a sense of control, and even deal with loss and grief. Maybe Toby helping others with their issues and their loss and grief will help him with his own issues."

Looking up over the top of the newspaper, Chris said, "Maybe."

"Animals can also help with the treatment of mental health problems. When I worked on the psychiatry unit in Fort McMurray, I don't recall us having access to a therapy dog, but I can think of at least a dozen patients that this could have made a significant difference with. Look how much Dooks helped the kids at the drop-in center in Lac La Biche when I worked there."

Getting my coffee and my papers, I kissed Chris on his forehead and went to continue my research. Toby headed outside.

Sitting at the desk in our home office, I looked out the window and glimpsed Toby showing off his fetching skills for the kids on the block. They pitched their Frisbee over the fence, and Toby tore after it, executed a graceful turn when he caught it, and loped back to the fence, where he stood on his hind legs to hand the Frisbee back to the kids. Whenever they called his name, Toby barked back, excited.

He didn't always show confidence in new situations, but otherwise he was perfect Chimo material. I was sure Toby could make a profound impact in people's lives, and perhaps others would make a similar difference in his life— and, by extension, ours.

After submitting our application, we secured an interview with the Chimo volunteer coordinator and tester. She gave us a package of documents, including examples of what the tests would look like and how we could help Toby prepare. We were told there would be three rounds of testing: an obedience test, a temperament test, and a health check. Just as at the first test, barking would not be tolerated. People would crowd him, yell, pet him in a clumsy manner, and hug him too tightly, and he would have to stay calm.

We began the training and homework exercises immediately, and Toby loved them, embracing the challenge. I admired how he stuck with learning something until he got it, no matter how many times he had to repeat the task. There were times when Christopher and I grew frustrated, but failure wasn't an option for Toby. His positive attitude toward the training kept us going until he'd mastered everything.

The testing environment was similar to the first place he'd tested. However, this time, Toby was the only dog being tested, so there were fewer people and less talking—and barking. Chris laughed at my nervousness. "It's not the end of the world if he doesn't pass, Charmaine. We don't even know if having a job is going to change his behavior."

"I know. I also know that *not* having a job has *not* changed his behavior. Anyway, I think my ego is invested in this now. I know Toby is smart enough to pass this test. I know he'd make a great therapy dog. I want the testers to know it, too." I adjusted Toby's collar and had to laugh at myself. "I feel a bit like a mom whose kid is in a beauty pageant."

I acted a lot like a proud mom when they told us Toby had passed. "Wasn't he great?" I enthusiastically asked strangers, who, to their credit, assured me that he was superb. Toby caught my excitement and began wriggling and jumping around. You would think he'd won the lottery—and understood what a lottery was.

Finally, Toby bolted toward a laundry basket full of dog toys. He'd eyed it each time we'd passed it during the test, but surprisingly, he didn't let it distract him from his tasks. I made a mental note: "Focus, clarity, and spirit." At the time, I didn't know why I etched these words in my mind, except that it was becoming clear that Toby was an inspiration to me. Later, when I was working on my own purpose and career, I would discover just how much Toby had motivated me that day.

Christopher was happy, too. "Maybe you'll finally stop tearing the bathroom apart," he said, scratching Toby under the chin before opening the door to the back seat of the car for him. "You'll have better things to do than drive us crazy."

Then he stopped and touched his head to Toby's as Toby stood on the seat. "Good job, buddy," he said quietly, while giving Toby what we called a royal back scratch. Toby's tail was going a mile a minute, and he quivered all over. You could almost see the joy streaming off him. Tears in my eyes, I turned away, giving my boys the bonding space they needed.

Seventeen

Chimo R Us

Several weeks passed before Toby received his first Chimo assignment. "It's at a mental health hospital," the volunteer coordinator said over the phone. I tried to write the information down while keeping my balance as Toby nudged at my legs. "The unit that he's being considered for sounds like a good fit for Toby. He'd be part of their recreation program, helping the patients get involved with recreational activities."

That did sound perfect. Deep down, I had worried about Toby being placed in a unit where he would be required to visit patients quietly. Sitting still was not his strong suit, and I wanted his first assignment to be a great experience for both him and the people he'd be helping. Being involved in a recreational program would allow Toby to be himself.

After hanging up, I bent down and looked Toby in the eyes. "Okay, Tobes, this is it. Are you ready?"

He barked once.

The following Wednesday, I put Toby's special red bandanna, which he had come to associate with "work," around his neck. Strutting up the steps of the hospital, head held high, he seemed to know he was doing something important. He was confident and well behaved, a dog on a mission, as we stopped at Reception.

He immediately became the center of attention. As we proceeded from Reception down the hall to the office of the volunteer coordinator for the hospital, Sharon, people poked their heads out of their offices and smiled when they saw Toby. Toby was, of course, curious about everyone and happy to return every hello, stopping to poke his nose into each office as we walked down the hall.

After an enthusiastic initial greeting with Sharon and an attempt to get her to play fetch, Toby settled down and seemed to be listening closely as she talked to me.

She explained the volunteer policies at the hospital and described Toby's role. As badly as I wanted Toby to get the job, I thought I should forewarn Sharon. "Toby does have a loud bark, and it can startle people. But he barks out of excitement not aggression. He's very gentle, loving, and playful."

I waited nervously for her response. I didn't have to worry. Sharon was the kind of person who looked for the opportunity in every situation. "We'll make sure the unit staff know about his barking," she said calmly. "An excited bark might just get people excited themselves about going outside to play with him. It might also give patients an opportunity to help Toby . . . who knows, this experience might be like therapy for the therapy dog." I hadn't thought about that before—this experience could benefit Toby in ways I had never considered.

"Getting people excited is one of Toby's gifts," I said. "He'll get people up and moving, no problem. He's passionate about playing and retrieving, and both will encourage patients to be more active."

"That's what we want. Now, are *you* ready for this?"

Her question took me by surprise. Of course I knew I'd be accompanying Toby during his duties, but I'd been so focused on his role and making sure he was comfortable and knew what to do that I hadn't given any thought to my participation.

My surprise must have showed on my face. Sharon smiled. "Let me guess. You haven't really thought about it. A lot of people don't. So why don't I tell you a bit about what to expect?"

I nodded.

"This hospital is for people with severe or ongoing mental illnesses. Many of our patients are here for the long term. Some come and go, whenever their conditions worsen and they need to stabilize or, sometimes, just to give their caretakers some respite. Some are here voluntarily; others have been ordered to be here.

"We try to keep our patients busy and give them a range of activities and programs to explore in addition to their treatment. So we have a lot of recreational activities, like sports programs and art programs, dances, and so on. We also arrange trips into the community for shopping or to go to a museum or to attend community events. And we teach skills that can be used in the workforce. Our patients often work in our coffee shop and car wash."

I nodded. "I'm very comfortable with this, Sharon. For a couple of years I worked with Alberta Mental Health and also worked on the psychiatry unit in a hospital. I developed programs for patients and an emergency crisis response service for the hospital and community. I really enjoyed working in that type of setting. Also, my university degree and college diplomas were in conflict analysis and management, social work, and social development.

"I'm looking forward to this. More than that. I'm excited about doing this for myself as well as for Toby."

"That's what I want to hear," said Sharon.

After explaining that I would need to go through a criminal record check, numerous reference checks, an orientation, and blood tests before we could start, Sharon said good-bye.

Leaving the hospital, I looked at everything around me with new eyes. This place was going to become important in Toby's life *and* mine. I had given plenty of thought to how Toby's new job would change him. But how would affect our household as a whole? How would it affect Chris?

And what about me?

Two weeks later, Toby was on the job. The security department was our first stop. Both Toby and I needed to get our volunteer security badges. As usual, Toby attracted attention. Security personnel crowded around him. Someone asked how he was in front of a camera—they had to take our photos, which would go on our badges. "Can you get him to face the camera?" With so many people around, I wasn't sure, although Toby was usually a complete ham for the camera.

Again, I didn't have to worry. A born performer, he put on a show for the camera. Everyone laughed as Toby vamped and showed off his brilliant smile.

New security badge clipped on his collar, red bandanna around his neck, special harness around his chest—Toby was ready for duty. I clipped on his red embroidered Chimo vest to make the working uniform complete.

We started walking through the hospital. Toby was curious but also a bit nervous. So many new smells, different noises, and places to explore. "It's okay, Toby," I said, "you're a good boy." People smiled, stopped, and greeted Toby as we passed. Of course, he interacted in his gentle way with everyone we encountered.

A walk that should have taken three minutes turned into a long journey. We were even a few minutes late arriving at the unit where we were to work.

Several patients sat around the room and looked up at us with little expression—an unusual situation for Toby. It was quite a somber atmosphere.

But the recreation therapist who approached brought a big smile with her. "Hi, Charmaine, I'm Terry. This must be Toby. Welcome. We're really excited to have you two join us." Next came the team we would be working with: Drell and Sarah. Toby took to them instantly. They welcomed us, bent down to pet Toby, and introduced themselves to him. The patients were still quiet, watching us.

"How was Toby's walk through the hospital to get to the unit?" asked Terry.

Before I could respond, Toby attempted to join the conversation. His bark rang through the unit like a gunshot. I tensed as everyone in the room jumped and turned to see where the unexpected noise had come from. Had Sharon forgotten to warn them? Were we going to be fired in our first two minutes on the job?

Then I noticed something amazing. The mood and energy in the room had changed. People were talking, smiling, and pointing at Toby. A room that a moment before had felt spiritless and flat now buzzed with curiosity and excitement. And possibility.

Toby's response to this shift in energy was interesting: he became quiet and pressed close to me. The staff introduced me and Toby, and I let everyone know that he was friendly, despite his big bark. I told everyone that Toby's barking was his way of communicating with them.

Sure enough, when introduced to each of the patients, his greeting was a loud bark. Although this startled and scared a few patients, most seemed perfectly comfortable with him. In fact, one patient was so pleased to see Toby that she greeted him repeatedly with his name, and he matched her excitement. Interesting, I thought.

I was peppered with questions about Toby: his age, likes and dislikes, his physical characteristics. Although the recreation program wouldn't begin until next week, Toby was already making a difference, inviting conversation and giving people the chance to engage with one another.

I admired how with each patient we approached, Toby seemed to be completely in the moment and fully present. After the introductions, he went around intentionally seeking particular people out, nudging them, wagging his tail and making eye contact. I was reminded of how important pure and unconditional attention and acceptance was.

Toby seemed to fill a void for people that we, as humans, were not able to do.

He followed every direction I gave him. At last Toby saw me as a pack leader. He definitely looked to me to be the lead, needing my guidance and reassurance. He let people pet him, yet was fully respectful of those who were not interested or were afraid of him. He seemed to know what to do and how to approach each individual, but he still wanted confirmation that he was doing the right thing. Talk about teamwork! From that moment on, I was a better "team" member with Chris, with friends, and in teaching the importance of it in my work with others.

"Can I pet him?" A middle-aged woman in a wheelchair sat some distance from the rest of the group. Her head was cocked and strawberry-blond hair streaked with gray covered her face, so at first I wasn't sure she was the person who had spoken.

But Terry knew. "Why, Anne, of course you can."

Anne shook her head, a slight movement evident only in the motion of her hair.

"Come on, Toby." I began to move toward Anne.

"Oh, are you leaving?" another patient asked.

"No, we'll be right back. Toby just wants to say hi to everyone today," I explained.

While Toby sat beside Anne's chair, Terry, Sarah and Drell began telling the other patients a little bit about Toby, drawing their attention and increasing the comfort level in the room.

Toby gave Anne a few polite sniffs. Head still lowered, she raised a hand and ran it across Toby's smooth head and neck. He nuzzled her hand and licked her wrist. Anne smiled.

"He likes you," I said.

There was no response. Anne was not interested in what I had to say. She was focused on Toby, even peeking up to look up at him through her hair. "You're a nice dog," she whispered finally, lowering her hand back into her lap.

Toby and I rejoined the group. When I looked up a few moments later, Anne was gone.

When our two hours ended, we went around the unit with the team to say our good-byes. Strolling down the hall, I glanced at Toby. What was that white powder all over his back? Dandruff—a common stress reaction for dogs. So this hadn't been as easy for him as he'd made it look. A couple of patients noticed me brushing the powder from his back. When I explained that Toby was a bit nervous because he was in a new situation, just as they would be if they were moving to a new unit or starting a new job, they were interested. They seemed to like that Toby faced the same kinds of challenges they did.

"Maybe we can help him get better," someone suggested.

I agreed and added that although Toby was a therapy dog, he was here as part of his own therapy, too. "He also has a problem with barking indoors," I told them. "I'm hoping that you guys will be able to help him stop that. Therapy for the therapy dog."

They liked that. When the patients said that maybe they could help Toby, I became aware of how powerful and meaningful this relationship between pet and patient could be.

"So Wednesdays with Toby will work for you both?" Terry stood in front of us, looking pleased.

Wednesdays with Toby. It sounded like a book title. "Absolutely," I said. "We look forward to it." Turning to go, I remembered something. "Wait—we didn't say good-bye to Anne."

"I meant to say something about that," said Terry. "That was incredible."

"What do you mean?"

"Anne has really isolated herself and hasn't spent much time out of her room since she got here two months ago. She certainly hasn't interacted with many people. But she was so vocal and confident around Toby . . . I can't believe that happened."

I was astounded. I met Toby's eyes.

"Toby," I said. "I knew you had it in you."

Eighteen

Wednesdays with Toby

Several weeks later, Toby came into my office around eleven thirty on a Wednesday morning. I was working on my presentation for a human resources conference later that week and wanted to finish before Toby and I left for the hospital. There were would be some two hundred people at the conference, where I was presenting on one of my favorite topics: Igniting Resilience. This presentation included my signature story, the sailboat accident. Since getting Toby, I had also blended in lessons about resilience that I had learned from the experience of having such a dog. The inclusion of Toby in the program had brought very positive feedback.

As my fingers clicked away on the keyboard, Toby parked himself beside me . . . and stared. Wrapped up in my writing, I gave him an absent-minded pat. He nudged my arm. I ignored him. He nudged again.

"Toby, I'm trying to write. What are you doing in here, anyway? It hasn't been ninety minutes." Toby was big on work/life balance. Staring and nudging were his ways of saying "Enough already. Let's have some fun." If I ignored his requests, which typically came after I'd been working for about an hour and a half, he would scoot under the desk, put his head on my lap, and push. Often I'd find myself rolled into the kitchen. It was funny, but it made getting work done harder than it needed to be.

But this time I'd been at the computer for only forty-five minutes and still had a lot to get done.

"Go play with your toys." I turned back to my work and didn't notice him leave and return until a Frisbee was shoved onto my lap, followed by a Kong—the two toys he cannot live without and which always come to the hospital with us.

I called Christopher at work. "Toby's trying to hurry me along for volunteering." I was practically whispering, sure that Toby could understand me. "He knows today is the day. Isn't that almost too weird?"

"Maybe he sees you getting ready, and he knows."

"No, I never get his knapsack out or make any preparations at all until it's time to go. He'd drive me crazy if I let on it was Wednesday."

There was silence on the other end of the line. "You're right. That's almost too weird."

Toby sat in front of me, staring, his tail thumping the floor—his version of a person impatiently tapping his foot.

Each week brought changes. At the hospital, Toby got better and better at intuitively knowing who to greet and cheer up and who needed space. The patients changed, too, demonstrating growth and improvement thanks to Toby's unconditional love. And I grew as well, changing my work schedule to accommodate our Wednesday afternoon visits. At home, the destructive incidents were in decline, although the closet was still emptied several times monthly.

I realized that for many people, managing a mental illness is something like living with Toby. You try different solutions and find that things are better one week—but then, inexplicably, decline the next. One step forward, countless steps back. It can be frustrating for patients and the people who love and care for them.

But Toby had no expectations for improvement in anyone's disposition or functioning. He didn't care if people got better. He just wanted to play and go for walks. It only made sense that patients gravitated toward him and relaxed in his company.

Anne, in particular, began to blossom. On our fourth visit, I found her in the lounge, sitting apart from the others but clearly making an effort to be part of the group. Her head was bent, but her hair was tucked neatly behind her ears, and when Toby and I drew closer, she looked up and smiled at him. Toby ran straight to her and shoved his head under her hand, then gazed at her adoringly as she stroked him.

"Toby's going to take some people outside to play ball today," Terry told Anne. "Feel like joining him?"

Anne's blue eyes, shining with joy a second before,

clouded over. "I don't like it outside," she said softly. "Stay in with me, Toby."

"It's beautiful out," Terry said. "The sun is shining. You don't have to play. You can just watch."

Anne shook her head vehemently. As our group marched out, she watched us leave, looking sad, but later I glimpsed her smiling face at the lounge window, watching Toby race after the Kong.

I started to record Toby's antics so we could discuss them with the patients every week. These discussions gave the patients opportunities to engage in conversation, provide ideas, and make suggestions for helping Toby. They loved to hear the weekly updates, and their confidence grew as they became more comfortable offering suggestions and helping Toby practice new commands and tricks. I noticed that the patients also showed concern for him from week to week; for example, one week after he had hurt his leg running after the Kong, the patients all inquired about how his leg was feeling during the week and what we had done to care for him.

One Wednesday, the unit supervisor asked if we would visit one of the patients in his room. Did I think Toby would be okay with going into a hospital room?

"Sure," I said, "he should be fine. He doesn't spend a lot of time in patients' rooms, but I think he'll do okay."

The supervisor broke into a relieved smile. "This gentleman has terminal cancer," she said. "He's here because he has no family, and he knows the staff and patients on this unit. He's declining rapidly, and we frequently hear him call out for Skipper, a dog he had many years ago. I know Toby isn't Skipper, but I thought that being with Toby might give him a few minutes of comfort."

Standing outside the man's door, tears sprang to my eyes. I was not unfamiliar with illness and death. I had worked in hospitals and had personally lost several loved ones to cancer. My grandfather had died just months before. I knew that death was a natural process and nothing to fear. What tore at me was thinking of the man's loneliness, dying in a hospital with no family to hold his hand or caress his face as he left this world. No one to share a childhood memory with him or to offer the comfort of touch in a painful or frightening moment.

Suddenly, I remembered something I had read, and that Maggie had told us several times about Toby. Toby was very intuitive and picked up on my emotions easily, which contributed to his anxiety. He was probably already anxious about entering the hospital room; he didn't need to worry about my sorrow, too. Taking a deep breath so he wouldn't sense an emotional change in me, I led him into the room.

"Toby, come in, come say hello. Good boy," I murmured as we walked to the bedside. The air was almost unbearably warm. The sound of labored breathing filled the room along with the beeps of medical equipment, and sure enough, Toby looked antsy and uncomfortable, pacing and staring at the door, tugging lightly on his leash. Still, I led him onward. The man in the bed was obviously fading fast, a poor shrunken figure topped with a shock of downy white hair. Toby's eyes met mine, and I saw his fear. *Please, get me out of here.*

Instead, I smiled at him. "Let's say hello, Toby," I whispered. He tugged toward the door again. Was I being cruel to ask him to do this? The patient's eyes were closed; he didn't know we were here and wouldn't miss us if we left. I glanced at Toby, then back at the bed, trying to decide what to do.

This time Toby followed my glance toward the bed. He stopped tugging on the leash and moved closer to the bed. As he approached, the man opened his eyes. Toby stopped, and for a moment the two of them looked at one another. Then, carefully, Toby placed his head on the patient's bed in a spot where the man could continue to look into his eyes.

With great effort, the emaciated man lifted a trembling hand and stroked Toby's head and nose. I held my breath. Toby did not like people touching his head or nose and would always politely move away after a second. But this time he just stood there. Only I knew how much this interaction was costing him, how uncomfortable he was.

"Skip . . ." The word wasn't much more than a sigh. The man gazed at Toby with what could only be described as love, his brown eyes warm with life as he recalled the memory of a dog he had loved with all his heart. Toby looked right back at him. Then, moving with great care, Toby tilted his head and gently licked the man's hand. From the bed came a gasp of joy, the purest sound I had ever heard.

The man's eyes glistened. I too was crying. Finally, the man looked at me and whispered his thanks. I could only nod, the lump in my throat too big to squeeze speech around, and the crescendo of feelings within me too huge to fit into words. I patted his hand.

And on shaking legs, led Toby from the room.

Nineteen

Gifts of the Heart

Toby's job was making a huge difference to both the patients and to him. At home, his behavior grew better each week, with less jumpiness or need to shadow me and Chris. At the hospital, each week brought new break-throughs and moments of amazement and joy that I was blessed to be a part of. It always surprised me how Toby simply knew what patients enjoyed and needed from him and how he adapted to work with each individual. Some patients' mental health changed from week to week; Toby simply stepped into whatever role was required that day. He also began to engage the patients in play with him. He would fetch, return, and drop a toy at their feet, rotating amongst the patients evenly to get everyone involved. If a new patient joined in later, he would run to that individual and drop the toy, barking until they got in the game.

The staff certainly saw the difference Toby made. They began to track patient activities before and after a visit with Toby. Terry mentioned that they were noticing that activity and socialization increased on "Toby's days." On Wednesdays, it was not unusual to see patients start to gather in the common area of the unit before Toby arrived. I wondered if the patients realized that Toby was helping them. I knew they enjoyed hearing about his quirky behaviors from week to week, including his more disastrous behaviors from the past, like breaking toilet tank lids, chewing fences to escape, and emptying closets and bookshelves. When Toby had a new episode, like sitting in the sink, I would be sure to tell the patients all about it. One patient pointed out that Toby was just like her: "Clumsy, gets the room messy sometimes, and does stuff that bugs other people." These kinds of comparisons were helping patients become more accepting of themselves.

I decided to ask them how they felt about Toby and what Toby did for them.

Amil was my first interviewee. A gentle but strong young man who greeted Toby's arrival at the hospital each Wednesday with a heartfelt smile and huge bear hug, Amil actually picked Toby up off the ground sometimes. Toby didn't mind.

"I was in bed, and I heard Toby barking so I got up and got dressed and came out," he said proudly.

"That's great. Toby is really energetic today and could use some of your Olympian toy-tossing skills to burn off some energy." We walked down the hall to join the group in the lounge. "Amil, how do you see Toby's role here at the hospital? What's his job?"

Amil replied with great confidence. "He brings happiness to those of us who are depressed and lonely because we're here in the hospital."

I could not have said it better. I felt as if Amil had just passed me a beautifully wrapped gift.

There were more gifts to come. A few minutes later, I spoke with another patient, one who was now enjoying Toby because he'd stopped barking so much and who seemed more relaxed and better able to carry on a conversation when Toby was around. "He's handsome," she said. "He knows how to handle himself when he's calm, but has a loud bark. He likes to stay with the people here. He helps me and likes to play around with people."

The staff joined in the discussion. One of the occupational therapists pointed out that Toby also seemed to benefit a great deal from being at the hospital. "I think Toby gets a feeling of fulfillment from this work. He teaches people that everyone has things they can improve on. He teaches patience and tolerance, and this is such an important life skill for patients . . . in fact, for all of us."

I had noticed this, too, and had discovered that the benefits Toby received from volunteering helped him make an even bigger impact. People have a hard time asking for help, not just in the hospital, but in life in general. Seeing that Toby also needed help made it easier for some patients to ask for and accept help from others.

This was a good lesson for me, too. I was very good at avoiding what I thought of as "the ask." I would struggle through a task, determined that I could and would manage it on my own without asking for help. Thinking about my relationship with Chris, I reflected on the many times I should have asked for his support or assistance but did not do so until I had no other option. The result was usually unnecessary struggling and frustration. Before Toby came into my life, about the only thing I'd willingly asked Chris for help on was with my master's degree statistics course. Talk about having no option . . . math was not my strong suit, and having Chris's help played a huge role in me doing fairly well in the course.

But lately, I realized, I'd learned to speak up and say what I needed. Toby's behavior had driven me to ask for help, advice, feedback, information—and, on occasion, forgiveness. And I was happy that it had. I liked knowing that support was there when I needed it; that I didn't have to handle everything on my own. It was a relief, really, to be able to just ask.

Outside at the hospital, Toby watched Amil with excitement. The big man held on to the Kong's rope and swung it above his head a few times while Toby circled him, barking and jumping. He knew the command "circle," and would run around you each time you gave the order, something the patients enjoyed. Finally Amil released the Kong, and as it flew through the crisp winter air, Toby took off after it, his eyes glued to the toy soaring overhead. Patients in the other units knocked on the windows and waved to Toby as he sprinted past.

"Wow, great throw, Amil!" I said. "It's almost in the next field. This will calm him down in no time."

Anne, who had gradually become more self-confident

and bolder, now sat outside to watch Toby play. She normally had a very soothing effect on Toby, so after about ten high-powered hurls, she suggested that Toby lie down. But he was too interested in the game to pay attention.

Anne became quiet and looked sad. "He won't listen to me," she said.

I looked at her. Pet-assisted therapy dogs like Toby help reinforce communication skills. Patients gain confidence as they become comfortable speaking assertively to animals and seeing the animals react positively. These skills can be transferred to interactions with other patients, family, and hospital staff, so that patients are able to speak up for themselves and develop healthy relationships. But it can be difficult for patients to discern between harshness and assertiveness, so it helps to coach them as they communicate directions to Toby. This type of mentoring came naturally to me. I had mentored and instructed thousands of people on communication skills.

"You know, the funny thing about dogs is that sometimes they pay more attention to *how* you say something than to *what* you say." Anne turned to me. "What if we practice telling Toby to lie down in a firmer voice and see what happens?" Anne looked uncomfortable. "Don't worry," I said, "Toby won't think you're angry. In fact, he'll appreciate understanding what he needs to do. When we don't use a firm voice, it's harder for him to know what's expected of him, and he can get confused."

I modeled this, calling Toby in a firm voice. He bounded over, eyes wide, tail wagging, and tossed his toy at us. "Good boy, Toby," I said, showing Anne that praise should be given in a different tone of voice than commands.

Toby barked twice. *Thank you.*

"Now you try," I said.

Anne called him five or six times, using her usual tentative and quiet voice. She became frustrated when he did not respond. "Toby, come. Toby. Come on. Toby, why aren't you listening? Come on." Toby, preoccupied with the toys and a new patient who had come to join the fun, ignored her. To him, her soft voice sounded like background conversation, nothing he needed to pay attention to.

I leaned over and whispered to Anne, "How about if you say: 'Toby! Come!' Make sure you look right up and speak with a voice that is firm. Don't worry. He won't think you're being bossy or mean."

Anne turned toward Toby. "Toby!" He turned his head and focused on her. "Come!" She patted the side of her leg. After glancing at Amil, Toby ran to Anne and sat at her side. I whispered a suggestion to praise him, and Anne rubbed his head. "Toby, good boy. You listened to me. It worked."

She gently pushed down on his rear end in an attempt to get him to lie down. Toby stiffened, barked, and nudged her.

"Anne," I said, "I think he needs help understanding what you'd like him to do next."

"I want him to lie down." Hearing the last two words, Toby dropped onto his belly.

"Wow . . ."

The staff members were smiling as they watched Anne sit up taller, confidence soaring. She thought she was telling Toby what to do; little did she know that at the same time, Toby was coaching her to be assertive and to communicate clearly.

Throughout our time at the hospital that day, the staff and I sought out opportunities for Anne to practice her communication skills with Toby. Toby responded in a way that showed he was helping her. Each time she lowered her voice and gave a command meekly, he ignored her. As soon as she put strength behind her words and explained her desires clearly, he did exactly as she asked. This interaction also solidified some of the speaking points I used in my presentations. For years I have explained in my seminars that how you say something is more important than what you say. But using Anne's experiences as an example seemed to give the information new meaning. It became something that everyone could relate to.

As a consequence of all this, Chris and I started teaching Toby to follow hand signals and whispered commands, so he could still respect a firm command but in a quiet voice. Both Toby and the patients benefited when Toby followed their instructions, so we found new ways to train Toby to ensure this would happen.

The next week while we were playing outside, I overheard Amil ask Anne for some of her candy. Normally, Anne would mumble that she didn't have very much, and Amil would ask again and again until she gave in and handed some over. This time was different. Looking him right in the eye, Anne said, "No." Her voice was loud and firm. Amil immediately walked away, in search of someone who didn't have Anne's ability to stand up for herself.

I smiled at Toby. He ran and dropped a toy in Anne's lap. *Congratulations.*

After allowing Anne to throw the Kong toy once or

twice, Toby decided it was someone else's turn. He nudged the Kong toward Sam and barked. Like Amil, Sam had a strong throwing arm, but Sam rarely spoke. The toy went so high that Toby lost it against the sun. "It's better when he focuses on the smell of the toy," said Sam. "Next time let's make him do that."

Sarah looked over at us in surprise. Encouraging Sam to socialize was an ongoing part of life at the hospital, but had been a slow process. "How are you going to do that, Sam?" she asked.

The whole group was interested and waiting to hear the answer. Sam stood a little taller, proud that he had information others wanted to hear. "In the wintertime, Toby kept losing his toy in deep snow because he couldn't see it. So I told Charmaine to rub it with a hot dog and then Toby wouldn't have to see it; he could smell it."

"It worked well," I said. "I still do that when I take him to the park."

Everyone murmured appreciatively as Sam beamed. A patient named Eleanor tilted her head and whispered for Toby to come to her. Knowing Eleanor's generosity and penchant for giving treats, Toby ran to her. I followed, my eye on Eleanor's hand. Last week she had snuck Toby a granola bar and some chocolate.

"Oh no, Eleanor," I said. "Thank you, but Toby does not want a cigarette. He would probably love a cuddle, though."

Eleanor looked affronted. How could we refuse her generosity?

"Eating that will make Toby very sick," I said. "I don't mind when you give him a carrot or some of his own special treats, but cigarettes are not good for him. Thank you for being so thoughtful of Toby." Eleanor's generosity—she was always offering gifts not only to Toby but to other patients, staff members, and guests—was admirable, but she needed to develop boundaries.

I made a mental note to bring a bag of Toby's goodies for her the following week—but Terry, Drell, and Sarah were already on it. To Toby's delight, they arranged a baking program where the patients made Toby some healthy dog treats. The treats were baked with love, and Eleanor noticed with pride how he gobbled them down: "He doesn't even chew them. He just wolfs them down in one bite."

Twenty

What a Difference!

There was no doubt about it: Toby had a knack for helping patients—Carolyn with her self-awareness and self-esteem; Sam with his socialization; Anne with her confidence; Marnie with getting over her fear of dogs . . .

For the first year, Marnie pretty much avoided Toby. But one day, she asked the nurse to bring him over. I walked Toby to where she sat in a big reclining chair. Marnie was a quiet middle-age woman, who often kept herself apart from the group and frequently talked softly to herself. Her condition changed quite dramatically from week to week. Toby would listen to her with one ear perked. He knew when she was struggling, and on those days he tended to avoid her, noting her "stay away" body language.

Today was different. "Hi, Toby," she said, patting his head. "You are such a nice dog. Can I have some treats to give him?" she asked me, and I pulled the training treats from my pocket and placed them in her hand. She held them out to Toby. No doubt unable to believe his luck, Toby gently took them all, then continued to lick her hand. Marnie started laughing and asked for some more treats.

I worked with Marnie to give Toby one treat at a time. Then she learned to issue Toby instructions such as "sit," "lie down," and "shake a paw."

"Toby likes me," she said, eyes bright. "He's listening to me."

The following week, Marnie was waiting in the reclining chair when we arrived and was quick to greet Toby. "I missed you, Toby. Charmaine, how is his foot? I've been thinking about Toby's foot all week." He'd gotten a minor cut on his paw the previous week. Cuddling Toby with both arms, she whispered, "I'm not afraid of you anymore. . . ."

I felt pure gratitude to be a part of these beautiful, trans-formational moments. As the patients' trust, confidence, and comfort with Toby grew, my pride and respect for him grew at the same pace. So did Christopher's, as I regaled him with stories each week.

I was learning from the patients, too. One day, Carolyn gathered the courage to let me know that since Toby's bark-ing didn't bother the patients, I shouldn't let it bother me, either. "When you ask Toby to stop barking," she said, "it's like you're asking him to stop talking with you. He's just being Toby."

I found this comment quite enlightening. From then on, I relaxed more with Toby's barking . . . and so did everyone else.

Another lesson that the patients taught me was to

observe what Toby actually *did* more closely. One Wednesday, Miriam joined us in the lounge at the hospital. This was surprising; usually she liked to be on her own. She and Charlene were the dog whisperers of the unit, talking to Toby in their quiet voices. Toby always mirrored their energy; with them, he was docile. By now, Toby had learned through training, practice, and his experience with the patients to follow directions from both verbal and hand signals. When he was lively, he required a firm tone to respond to the direction; otherwise, even soft commands got his attention. I had discovered that above all, Toby needed *clear* commands.

On that day, we stayed in the visiting room for a change, playing indoors. Since we were in a small room, the usual soccer game soon turned into Toby in the Middle. "Get it, Toby," said Charlene as she gently kicked the ball to Sam. Sam tossed it to me, and I kicked it to Miriam. Suddenly everyone broke into laughter. "He's kicking the ball, Charmaine," said Miriam.

"He what?"

"He kicked the ball with his foot, he's copying our behavior."

She was right. Toby was imitating our actions and trying to kick the ball with his right front foot, or, if he wanted to send the ball backward, his right rear foot.

Suddenly I thought about Toby's annoying habit of following people into the washroom or of fleeing to that room and shutting himself in when he was scared. I'd always assumed the first behavior was due to his need to remain close to people and the second simply to his being a weird and extremely anxious animal. Could I have been wrong?

Could Toby simply be mimicking our behavior? People go into the washroom, so he goes into the washroom. People close the washroom door, so he closes the washroom door.

This was an entirely new way of looking at Toby's quirks.

Toby even helped the staff members. One day, Terry said, "This day is getting away from me. Toby, go wake up Miriam." The request made me laugh. Miriam was a middle-aged lady, very gentle and quiet, with a voice so soft you had to listen extra close just to follow her conversation. Around her, Toby was quieter than usual, too; just sitting there while she stroked his head and ears. Besides, although Toby was smart, I doubted he knew enough to trot down to Miriam's room and shake her from her sleep.

Still, holding the end of the leash, I walked Toby off to Miriam's room, curious to see what Toby would do—he rarely entered patients' rooms.

Terry opened the door and in Toby went, as if he had done this a hundred times before. He trotted straight to the bed and nudged Miriam several times, then licked her hand and face. She didn't respond. She had been through a lot lately and was quite depressed.

"Miriam, Toby wanted to say hi to you," said Terry.

When Toby discovered his efforts weren't working, he put two paws on the bed and leaned into Miriam, nudging her forcefully. She finally stirred, reached out a weak hand and stroked Toby. She smiled. Terry and I looked at each other.

When we were leaving, Miriam whispered, "Thank you, Toby."

Toby gave a quiet woof in return.

When Drell heard this story, he said, "Toby, we should

record your barking and use it as an alarm clock to wake everyone up."

"Maybe you should start coming in every day, Toby," Terry said. "If I get any busier, you can give me a hand doing the program schedule. How are you with paperwork?"

BFFs on the Beach

"Toby!"

"Come here, Toby!"

Each week, the calls rang out through the unit Toby had claimed as his own. Bounding in, he immediately took charge of the room, making his round of greetings, sniffing out those who needed extra attention that day. He was having the time of his life.

Over dinner, Chris asked how Toby did at the hospital that day.

"I wish you could see him there, Chris. Watching him connect with people is so moving. I just know that he is helping these patients in the most wonderful ways. It's a remarkable thing for Toby, too, that he is feeling so needed. I can just sense that he knows what he is doing is important and good."

I told him about a hospital employee who had always been afraid of Toby, moving far away from us until we had passed whenever came across her. "Last week she was at the vending machine, and I stopped to say hello. Toby went over to her and sat beside her and gently nudged her hand. She kind of gasped and then she just smiled and said hello to him. Later that day, she actually patted his back quickly when we passed by. He makes such a profound impact on people—even if I don't exactly know why or how, his being there helps them on some level. But I have the feeling it's more than he simply makes them happy in the moments he's there. He's developed bond with the patients . . . they need it, it seems. It is beautiful to watch and touches me so much."

Christopher nodded.

"Toby is meant for great things, Chris. I am absolutely certain of that."

"It sounds like he's already doing great things, Char. And I think he deserves a holiday. What do you think about running up to the cottage for a week?"

I thought it was a brilliant idea. Between dealing with Toby, my career, and now the emotional rollercoaster of volunteering, I felt like I'd been going full-tilt for a whole year. A week at my favorite place in the world to rest and recharge was exactly what I needed.

We loaded the truck on Saturday morning, the sky still pink and the birds pouring their hearts into celebrating a new day. As I handed Chris a cup of coffee, I pointed to Toby rolling in ecstasy on the dew-covered lawn. He shook his head. Nothing like the smell of wet dog in an enclosed vehicle first thing in the morning.

"Toby, let's go," Christopher called, holding the truck's back door open. Toby leapt in, wriggled around, squeezed through the gap between the front seats, and took what he considered to be his proper place behind the wheel. Chris opened the driver's door and tried to coax him. Toby gave him a puzzled look and panted happily, waiting for us to climb in and get started on whatever adventure was coming next.

In her letter to the rescue agency, Toby's previous owner had written that Toby, if instructed to do so, would obediently climb into the backseat, lie down, and sleep. We had never gotten him to do this except when he was left in the car to wait for us. Then we would return to find him snoring peacefully—in the driver's seat. He was very attached to being in the driver's seat. It was not uncommon for our ninety-pound animal to quietly creep up to the front seat and attempt to share the wheel while we drove.

But finally we were off, with Toby in the back, hanging his head out the window.

Lac La Biche, one of the many lakes in northern Alberta, is a two-hour drive from our home. As we covered the miles, I could feel the challenges and worries of everyday life dropping away. I couldn't wipe the smile from my face. I glanced at Christopher, relaxed behind the wheel. I couldn't see his eyes through his sunglasses, but his grin told me all I needed to know. I reached over and stroked his hair. Toby nosed in and rested his head on Chris's shoulder.

"What's this?" I said. "Hands off your Christopher?" I gave Toby a pat, too. He placed his head on my shoulder, then compromised by settling down with his head on the console. His favorite place: right between us.

The chalet-style home that we call our cottage is surrounded by beautiful old willows and sits right on the beach of the lake. We'd bought it fifteen years earlier and had made it our permanent home for a couple of years. It was during that time that we'd been swept off our Hobie Cat and, later, gotten married. Since then, we tried to spend as much of the spring and summer at the cottage as possible, usually taking our work along with us—but sometimes, like on this occasion, leaving all work behind. A true vacation.

As we turned onto the gravel road that would lead us to the house, we all felt a bit giddy.

"We're here!" I exclaimed as the peaked roof and glassed-in front porch of our home away from home came into view. Chris laughed at my excitement, and Toby, barking excitedly, rammed the front half of his body between our seats to get a better look.

"Toby!" I shouted, my ears ringing. Too excited to obey my command to shush, Toby barked some more and grinned at me. He adored being at the cottage; as a water dog and bird hunter, he was right at home in the lake, swimming after sticks and chasing birds. Unlike his foster owner David, we had never had to leap into the water to save him from drowning, but he had also never come close to catching a bird. He did take on a flock of geese once as they waddled from our neighbor's yard to ours, but quickly turned tail when the larger geese flapped their wings and honked at him. We laughed about his lack of guard dog skills as he came running back to us with his tail between his legs, the mighty hunter defeated.

But by far the biggest draw of the lake for Toby was his lakeside friend Lauren—a little neighbor girl with whom he spent hours upon hours playing. I glanced toward her cottage, three doors from ours, and saw the family car parked in the driveway. Dog and child were in luck. I wondered how long it would be before she made an appearance.

After opening the cottage and unpacking, we took our regular walk around, concluding with a stroll down the lane. Toby was carrying a dirty old tennis ball in his mouth.

As we approached Lauren's house, Toby ran up the driveway and stood at the front door. Then something to the right caught his attention, and, ears perked, he ran toward the garage. Again he sat and waited.

We didn't see anyone around. We called Toby, but he ignored us. There must have been someone in the garage, and Toby assumed it was Lauren. But I wanted to finish our walk, so I called firmly, "Toby. Come. Let's go."

It took several attempts, but finally Toby sauntered up the incline through the trees to the road. His mouth was empty.

"Where's your ball, Toby?" asked Chris. Toby sat down. Chris and I exchanged a questioning look.

"Toby, go get your ball. Get it." Toby whimpered but remained sitting. After several commands to retrieve the ball and Toby declining—which had become one hundred percent unusual for him—we continued our walk.

Eventually Toby joined us, trotting along behind without his tennis ball. Chris and I looked at one another. "He's left his ball for her," Chris said. "A calling card. He wants her to know he was there."

We continued our routine, the walk around the property, admiring how the garden was progressing, and then a stroll along the beach to enjoy the view and the birds. Toby especially loved the branches thronged with blue jays, yellow and red grosbeaks, a few long-tailed woodpeckers, and a little songbird Chris called the "cheeseburger bird" because its joyful cry sounded as if it were repeating "cheeseburger" over and over.

Filling our birdfeeders was the last part of our cottage routine. After that, Christopher and I parked ourselves in lawn chairs facing the water and relaxed. I raised my face to the sun. Chris settled down to read a book with a happy sigh. Somehow, there was never enough time for reading at home. Toby raced around on the beach, barking at birds and running in and out of the water before eventually collapsing between our chairs.

"Toby! Toby!" a child called. Sure enough, it was Lauren approaching at a full run, dressed in a blue wetsuit, pink water shoes, and goggles, a sand pail clutched in each hand. Toby jumped to attention, staring at her, his entire body vibrating with excitement, then he bolted toward her. The two collided in a huge, wriggling hug. I never tired of watching this magical reunion.

"Toby! You missed me, didn't you? You came to see me!" Lauren put down her buckets and reached into one of them. Out came the mangled tennis ball. "I knew it when I found this."

Chris and I looked at one another. The secret message had worked.

Lauren ran up and gave Chris a hug. "Hi, Big Squirt," she said.

Chris laughed and picked her up, lifting her high into the air. "Hi, Little Squirt." They'd used these nicknames for each other for years.

Next she gave me my hug. As I released her, I said, "Lauren, did I tell you that Toby knows your name? Whenever we say it, his ears perk right up, and he goes around the house looking for you."

Lauren grinned and looked at Toby, who let out three loud barks. *Yes I do.*

"That's because we're best friends," Lauren said. "Okay, Toby, we're going to the beach, and then we're going to have a tea party."

"He's not that much of a tea-party dog," I said, "but I bet he'd love it if you threw some balls for him to swim after."

I watched the two of them run into the water, Toby barking and Lauren squealing. A bright, sunny nine-year-old with a passion for pink, she shared a bond with Toby that was uniquely their own. Although Toby was rarely willing to leave Chris's or my side, he regularly snuck off to call on Lauren, peering into her family's kitchen through their sliding glass door and barking until Lauren came outside.

The two of them brought out the best in each other. Lauren had taught Toby tolerance, and how to put his head underwater—something he never did for Chris or me. For her part, Lauren was learning the value of friendship and spending time with those you love.

The previous summer, we had found a to-do list she had written to herself and left in our cottage. "Play with Toby from 1:00–2:00. Take pictures of things and email them to whomever from 2:00–2:30. Eat something healthy, have a shower, and call Mom 2:20–3:20. Play with Toby 3:20–3:40." Our refrigerator was covered with love notes to Toby from Lauren, carefully detailed drawings of Toby, and sticky notes reminding us to buy him a new toy or give him a special treat. She also left poetry:

Toby and Lauren are best buddys.
We are crazy about each other.
Sometimes Toby licks me wherever I get hurt.
We never hurt each other's feelings.
Toby is my BFF forever.

Toby and Lauren were kindred spirits, and I had begun to use the lesson of their relationship in my presentations, where I said their connection took place "at the heart level rather than at the head level." I suggested that if we related to our colleagues and clients in the same way, we would get better results and have more meaningful working relationships.

The power of a BFF. . . . I looked at Christopher, who had closed his book and was watching Toby and Lauren frolic in the sun. If there was one person I connected with on a heart level, it was he. And I realized I'd been taking him for granted. I leaned over, grabbed his hand, and brought it to my lips.

"What was that for?" He looked confused, but he was smiling.

"You know how Toby feels when he sees Lauren? That's how I feel when I see you."

It was time to have some fun with my own BFF.

Twenty-two

Letting Go

Our days at the cottage were spent swimming, sailing, working in the yard, and taking long walks while Toby ran circles around us, chasing sticks, birds, and insects. In the evenings, we often relaxed around a campfire by the water. Toby would fall asleep staring at the flames and embers.

We took the canoe out several times. Toby was a good passenger, sitting motionless, not rocking the boat. We didn't know if he was just trying to be helpful or scared stiff, maybe a little of both.

The canoe wasn't the only thing that Toby was afraid of, and one day he taught me an important lesson that had to do with looking fear in the face, mastering it, and moving forward.

While he loved the water and swimming, Toby was enormously fearful of diving from the dock. I watched him bolt down the long dock, picking up speed as he neared the end. Each time as he skidded to a near stop, he belly flopped into the lake. Each failed attempt to dive resulted in a growing fear. Then something sparked in Toby; he confronted his fear of diving. Watching him run full speed down the dock, he shot his front legs forward and hind legs backward; it was a perfect dive, surprising both himself and me. After swimming back the shore, he raced down the dock and dove again and again. In one day, he mastered the skill and overcame his fear.

That's remarkable, I thought. He's fearful and knows it, and he is demanding himself to work through this. What an incredible process he had taken to confront this fear; what an incredible skill, to be able to assess his fear and make a plan to work through it. Immediately, I knew that I had seen Toby do something that I wanted to do more of myself—readily confront my own fears, overcome them, and move forward.

Certainly Chris seemed to do this better than I did. After all, the day following our life-threatening sailing experience, Chris found our sailboat with the help of the Royal Canadian Mounted Police (RCMP), and he got back on the boat. I, on the other hand, looked at the boat with fear and distrust. These feelings were so intense that I allowed them to rule me. The following morning, I watched as Chris zipped up his life jacket, clipped the whistle to his vest, and checked all the lines.

"Come on Char, are you coming? It's a good day for a sail; the wind's not too strong."

Looking at the boat, I said "Maybe next time, Chris."

The summers that followed were just the same; "maybe next time" became my mantra to avoid my fear of sailing. Chris continued to sail the boat alone. A disappointed Chris said, "Char, you've been saying that for three years. Nothing bad will happen. You have to trust that. You have got to work through this fear."

"I do trust you, Chris!" Where did that come from, I wondered.

Not convinced, Chris said, "I don't think you do. That's why I offered to have someone else give you sailing lessons, to help you build your sailing skills and your confidence. You have to get over this fear."

Hoisting the sails, Chris asked one more time. "Char . . . you coming?"

Torn between fear and wanting to jump on the boat to show Chris, and myself, that I could do it, I quietly said, "Maybe next time, babe. Have fun." I watched Chris and the boat sail into the sun. Chris had confronted his fear, like Toby did with diving. I succumbed to fear, gave up instead of persevering, and missed out on three wonderful summers of sailing with Chris.

The fourth summer, Chris sold the Hobie Cat and bought a bigger but more stable sailboat. He removed the reminder of the old sailboat so that I could move forward. In an attempt to appease Chris, I hopped on the boat.

Watching Toby that day, never was it more clear. I knew I wanted to have more courage like Chris, getting on boat immediately, and like Toby, working though his fear and mastering the skill of diving.

Our cottage holiday was also turning out to be good for Chris's and my relationship. For the last year or so, Christopher and I had been busy in our work lives, and so preoccupied that we hadn't noticed how much we actually missed the "just us" time. Now we reconnected on a deeper level and were back to having fun.

Each morning I worked in my garden, planting seeds and bedding plants I had picked up in a neighboring town: tomatoes, lettuce, and peas we would eat straight from the soil and vine later in the season. The afternoons found me lying in the shade, a book in one hand and a cool drink in the other, Toby snoozing beside me.

And one evening, Christopher and I were invited by friends who lived next door to come to their home for a visit. Unsure about leaving Toby alone in our picture-perfect cottage—something we had not yet had the nerve to do—we put him on the enclosed porch. He'd spent hours that day playing fetch, running around, and swimming. Surely he'd just curl up and sleep. We'd be home before he even missed us. . . .

A mournful wail followed us as we walked through the warm evening air to the neighboring property.

"Don't turn around," ordered Chris.

A series of barks. Another wail.

"Oh, he sounds so sad."

"If he sees you turn around, he's going to start barking his head off."

I knew Christopher was right, and I resisted the urge until we got to the neighbor's front door. Then I pretended to scratch my ankle and stole a peek at our porch. Toby stood on his hind legs, his nose practically pressed to the window, gazing out at us.

Beside me, Chris laughed. He'd stolen his own peek. "That is tragic. That poor dog. We are the world's worst dog owners," he said.

An hour later, we returned to find every single item in the porch knocked over. Toby wriggled and leaped with joy in the middle of the chaos, apparently astounded that he was not going to be left alone, locked in a porch, for the rest of his life. Paw prints covered the windows on all three walls. Chris and I could only image Toby walking around the perimeter of the porch, frantically pawing at the glass, desperate to escape.

I awoke the next morning to a scene almost as disconcerting, in a very different way. For the past two years, a beautiful porcelain vase had rested on a windowsill in the living room. It contained Dooks's ashes. Dooks had loved the lake as much as Toby did, and after he died, we hadn't been able to completely part with the memories of him.

Now the vase sat on the floor. Miraculously, it was both unbroken and unopened, but there was no doubt how it had gotten there—it was positioned next to the sleeping Toby, almost touching his nose.

This sight took my breath away . . . and made me realize it was time for me to gather my courage and do something I'd been thinking about the entire time we'd been at the cottage.

As Chris and I took our morning stroll, coffee in hand, I broached the subject.

"Chris," I said, "I've been thinking. Remember when Maggie told us Toby didn't really understand his role in our family?"

Christopher nodded. "Mmmm hmmm."

"I think that that was—and still is—partly because, in our minds, we haven't completely stopped thinking of Dooks as the top dog in our family. Toby can't be the dog because Dooks is still around—even if only in spirit. We're hanging on to him, and I think Toby knows it."

"That makes sense." But Chris looked uncomfortable. I think he knew what I was going to propose.

"Honestly, we have just as many photos of Dooks on the fridge as we do of Toby. In fact, I just noticed that here at the cottage, we don't have any photos of Toby at all, but lots of Dooks. If it weren't for the pictures that Lauren has drawn, anyone walking in here would expect to find Dooks sleeping in a corner, not Toby."

Head down, Chris nodded.

"And then there are the ashes," I said. "Toby knocked the urn off its shelf this morning. He was sleeping with it."

"He was?"

"I don't know what made him do it, but it made me think . . . it's time to put Dooks to rest. I think we, and Toby, need that closure. I know Toby didn't even know Dooks, but I don't know . . . something just tells me that for Toby to grow, we have to let go of Dooks."

For a moment Chris said nothing. Then he nodded again and said, "You're right."

Later that afternoon, we took the urn down to the lake. Toby ran ahead of us toward the dock, stopping just short of the end, where he scanned the water for birds within catching distance. The sun was low in the sky and the water perfectly still, reflecting a sunset of rare intensity. Overhead, three groups of geese in perfect formation swept in from different directions, ready for an evening swim.

As the sun crept below the horizon, Christopher and I opened the urn and each took out a small handful of ashes.

Toby sat uncharacteristically still, watching us.

Speaking softly, my throat tight, I addressed the whole great universe as I recounted the pleasure and love Dooks had given us. "Sometimes you meet someone you know right away, that they were always meant to be in your life. Meeting you was like that, Dooks. You came into our home, into our lives, such a happy little white ball of fur . . . and within five minutes, I couldn't imagine my life without you. Every day with you was better than the day before, even those days at the end when you were in pain and couldn't do much more than gaze at us with eyes full of love. I'll never forget the way your beautiful coat felt when I stroked you. I'll never forget the way you smelled and how you loved to pull those old fallen branches out of the woods, dropping them at our feet so we'd throw them for you."

On and on I went, and when the memories were finally depleted, I wiped my tears, took a deep breath, and said, "Good-bye, my sweet Dooks." I released ashes over the water.

Without prompting, Christopher said, "Dooks, you were a wonderful dog. The best. I hope you're up there running free, chasing squirrels and rabbits. It was an honor to know you, buddy. Good-bye."

Opening his hand, Chris let Dooks's ashes dance in the breeze and settle onto the water, where they swirled in beautiful patterns.

I squatted to pet Toby, who licked away my tears. "Thanks, Toby. You're a good boy, and now you're our family dog, okay?"

Chris squatted, too. "You're lead pooch, now."

Did Toby understand what had just happened? It seemed impossible. I wasn't sure if even Chris and I understood or if this ceremony would allow us to let go of Dooks completely. But then I remembered Toby's depression after his owner died. Even he had had trouble accepting change and moving on, being able to love his next owner the way he'd loved the first. Death and loss were hard on everyone, man and beast.

As we walked back to the cottage, I thought about writing a letter to the woman who had given Toby up, to let her know how much we loved him and to reassure her that he was doing well and that I hoped she was.

The three of us then went into the garden, where I chose a spot to bury Dooks's remaining ashes. The perfect spot was right beside a salmon-colored bush that Dooks had marked as his own every time we arrived at the cottage. This bush was resilient, surviving many moves and harsh winters. Digging in the damp, heavy soil, my hand touched something furry. I jumped back with a shriek—then was relieved, and surprised, to see one of Dooks's stuffed animals.

The place I had chosen for Dooks had been his own choice, too.

The next day, we headed back, and although we knew we'd be back soon, this week had been special: we had officially christened Toby into the family.

In the days after our return, Toby was extremely well-behaved, almost like a normal dog. Or at least we hoped this would be so.

Back at work, it was as if Toby had never been away. He got right back into the swing of things, selecting the patients who needed him, raising the overall excitement level of the unit, coaxing patients to get out and play. At home, Toby's good behavior continued . . . for the most part. By Toby standards. But Christopher and I were happier than ever, and I renewed my focus on my career and prepared to enter a coaching program to help move my own skills to the next level.

Then came a Wednesday morning when I let Toby wait for me in the truck while I finished some phone calls before we left for the hospital. I had no premonition of disaster as I hurried to the garage, no sense of catastrophe as I opened the door of the truck . . . but then I saw Toby's face.

And then I saw the interior of the truck.

"Oh my gosh! Toby, what have you done?" The carpet was torn ragged, the spare tire cover had been yanked off and chewed up, and the plastic molding looked like an entire family of beavers had been working at it.

"I was only gone aa short time." I felt sick to my stomach. How would I break this news to Christopher? Why was it that every time I thought we'd gotten a handle on Toby, I discovered I had more to learn?

Twenty-three

A Star Is Born

"Look at this, Christopher. *Chicken Soup for the Soul* is doing a book of stories about the lessons people have learned from their dogs. Wouldn't Toby be perfect for that?"

Christopher was wrestling with Toby on the floor. "Toby? *This* dog? What did we learn from Toby, other than how to buy toilet tank lids in bulk and restock a closet in under a minute?"

"Ha, ha. With Toby, it's not just what we learned, but what he gives to others. I think his story would be a great addition to this book."

"Well, you're the writer, Char. You write speeches and training materials for your clients and presentations; you have a box full of journals. Go for it. It'll be the best story in the book."

I smiled at him. For the most part, Chris kept his emotions under wraps, but he never hid his pride in me. It was such a blessing to have a husband who believed that I could do anything I set my mind on. Someone who told me to go for it instead of listing reasons why I might not succeed.

Toby's story, which I called "Volunteering from the Heart," was easy to write; the words just seemed to flow from my heart to the paper. I enjoyed writing about Toby's accomplishments at the hospital and the difference he made in the lives of others. Recounting his not-so-good qualities wasn't as enjoyable, though. In fact, sometimes I felt like I was reliving a nightmare. But I knew I couldn't tell one side of Toby's story without telling the other. Besides, I had learned that there was entertainment value in the trials and tribulations Toby had put me through. Everyone, from the patients at the hospital to friends and family, loved hearing about Toby's escapades, and the wilder the stories, the better.

"There are really two ways of looking at everything, aren't there, Christopher?"

"What do you mean?"

"Take Toby's destructive outbursts, for example. We can look at them as terrible incidents—"

"Which we do." Christopher looked sternly at Toby, who was now cleaning a stuffed bear. Chris had still not completely forgiven Toby for destroying the interior of the truck, and only the previous evening Toby had locked himself in the washroom while Chris and I were gone to dinner—we'd forgotten to close the door. We'd returned to find him barking madly, the entire room a disaster zone. Although we had learned to live with such incidents, neither of us had been very happy about cleaning up a big mess at midnight. The time between Toby's fits was growing longer, but the disastrous moments still frustrated us.

"But we could also look at them as humorous tales," I said. "Conversational fodder."

"Sure. We could also look at them as cries for help. As we've done. Or as bouts of boredom. Which we've done. No matter how you look at them, they don't seem to stop."

"But that's my point. I just wonder if it isn't better to change how you perceive the situation, how you define it. I mean, if it isn't going to change anyway, why not enjoy it?"

Christopher rolled his eyes. Either I wasn't communicating clearly or he didn't want to hear what I was trying to say. Probably a little of both.

Within two months, I got a fax on official *Chicken Soup for the Soul* letterhead. "Dear Charmaine, Congratulations. Your story, 'Volunteering from the Heart,' has been selected to appear in *Chicken Soup for the Soul: What I Learned from the Dog*."

I read the letter aloud to Christopher several times and showed it to Toby. Then I stowed the letter, signed by Jack Canfield and his co-author, Mark Victor Hansen, in my keepsake file. I had admired Jack Canfield as a speaker and coach for many years; for me, having his signature was almost as exciting as getting Toby's story into the world.

The patients at the hospital were excited, too, partly because the story focused on Toby's volunteer work with them, but also because they loved Toby so much.

"Toby will be famous!" cried Amil. "I've never met a famous person before."

"You still haven't," said Christine. "Toby is a famous *dog*."

"He seems like a person to me," said Amil. Everyone else—including I—agreed with Amil.

When the books arrived, I was ecstatic. It was exciting to open the covers and see my story—Toby's story—in print. I read it several times, once aloud to Toby.

I wrote a story about Toby for the Chimo newsletter, and we decided to send out a press release about the *Chicken Soup for the Soul* story. I wanted to raise awareness of Toby's work at the hospital, and of pet-assisted therapy in general, and thought this would be the ideal way to garner some attention for these important services and organizations.

I also wanted to raise awareness about the importance and value of rescue agencies. Toby, the dog who needed teaching, was now becoming the teacher.

Several newspapers picked up and covered the story. One printed Toby's photo on the front page along with a half-page article; our local paper printed a three-quarter-page story featuring several photos of Toby, including one of him in his work uniform outside the hospital. Shortly after the stories ran, when we took Toby for walks, we were often asked if this was "Toby from the newspaper." Toby enjoyed the additional positive attention. Before we knew it, he had become something of a local celebrity.

His television debut was exciting for everyone who knew him. A reporter and videographer from a local TV station came to our home and conducted the interview in the little park we could access from our backyard. After three or four minutes of the reporter and me talking about Toby, Toby grew bored. He picked up his Kong toy and tossed it to the reporter, interrupting the interview but making everyone laugh. Showing the diva that lives within him, Toby also made a point of running straight up to the camera for a close-up. The program was a hit and aired several times, both locally and nationally. Across the country in Ontario, Toby's proud grandparents spread the news about their famous four-legged family member, Toby.

With Toby's name becoming so well known in the community, our local Chapters bookstore was very agreeable to hosting a book signing and paw-printing event. The manager made up colorful, attractive posters with Toby's headshot and the book cover, and not only displayed it in the store, but gave all the stores in the mall their own copy to display. Toby's smiling face was everywhere.

The day before the event, Christopher and I took Toby to Chapters to meet the staff and get familiar with his surroundings, as he'd never before been in a mall, much less a bookstore. His bark seemed loud and out of place there.

"I hope he's going to be okay tomorrow, Christopher," I said. "Four hours is a long time. . . ."

"He'll be fine. We'll just take him out every half hour or so to give him a break."

On the big day, we arrived about twenty minutes before the signing. A table had been set up by the front door, with a tablecloth, a pile of books, and cookies for guests. A line of people had already formed in front of the table. All the commotion made my stomach flip. This was really happening. I was overwhelmed with gratitude and joy and suddenly became aware of one of Toby's biggest gifts: his ability to connect me with my feelings on a new level. It was like he brought out the real, authentic me. I smiled down at Toby as he nudged my arm. *You finally get it, Mom.*

"Wow, Christopher," I said, "this is incredible." I couldn't believe so many people knew about Toby and cared enough to make a special trip to meet him. In fact, more than eighty people came to visit Toby that day, to have their book paw-printed or to shake his paw. Many had read about him in the *Sherwood Park News* and the *Edmonton Journal*. Others had read about him in a blog written by Jamie Hall, the pet writer for the *Edmonton Journal*. Some had seen him on TV. And some just couldn't resist following the barks that rang through the normally quiet bookstore. Little children yanked on their parents' hands to get to Toby. Chris did a great job of handling Toby; it was clear that he and Toby were finally on the same page.

For this event, Christopher and I had trained Toby to push down on a self-inking stamp with his paw. The stamp, specially created for the occasion, left a paw print and Toby's name on the paper. It was a lot easier and cleaner than pressing Toby's own paw on an inkpad would have been.

Watching Toby paw-print his first book, I laughed, but I was overwhelmed with emotion, too. This dog had once been so lost and bored and unsure. He'd spent most of his time tearing the house apart and destroying whatever he could get his paws on; now he used those same paws to carefully and expertly make his mark on the world in a positive way.

Of course, Toby added his personal touch to each "signing": two loud barks after each stamp. The crowd was delighted. For my part, I inscribed the books: "Play, work, and live with purpose!"

Busy signing books, greeting new people, and telling Toby's story over and over again, I didn't have time to look around the room for familiar faces. So I was surprised when Maggie took her place at the front of the line.

"Look at you, Toby. You're famous. But I always knew you would be." She scratched him under the chin, and he barked hello.

"He's doing so well today, Maggie," I said, "thanks to your training and advice. I don't know where we'd be if you hadn't helped us."

Maggie shook her head. "I pointed you in the right direction, that's all. Toby did the rest." She put her copy of the book in front of Toby and he stamped it, then watched Chris introduce Toby to new guests. "When I met Chris at your home the first time, it was obvious how frustrated and detached he was with Toby. Today he's like a proud father. I am so pleased for all of you."

"Thank you, Maggie. I—"

"Toby! Toby! Over here!"

I couldn't believe my ears. That was Amil's voice ringing through the bookstore. Then I saw him waving from the back of the line, pushing his way through.

"Can we just help this man first?" I asked the couple next in line. "He's a very good friend of Toby's." They agreed to wait, and I watched Amil approach. I was happy to see him—but, judging from the size of his smile, not half as happy as he was to see Toby. We'd just sign his copy of the book, say hi, and get back to the line again.

Except it wasn't just Amil. More of Toby's friends had arrived. Two of Toby's playmates from our neighborhood arrived bearing gifts—a new ball. They crowded around the table, calling to Toby, petting him, and admiring the book. Toby's barks split the air, and I noticed a few people in the queue covering their ears.

"This is not working," I whispered to Christopher, while smiling through clenched teeth at the visitors. It wasn't their fault that Toby was overexcited. He was just happy to see them. But we were all going to get kicked out if this went on.

"Toby, you're famous," said our neighbor. "Can I have your autograph? And look—we brought you a new ball."

Amil turned and addressed the people in the line up. "Toby is the smartest dog you'll ever meet. We're Toby's friends, and we know him really good, and you're lucky to get his autograph. Right, Toby?"

Hearing his name, Toby barked again. And again and again. People were starting to back up and look concerned.

Things were unraveling fast.

Twenty-four

Searching for Perfection in an Imperfect Dog

Luckily, it all worked out in the end. Once Toby's friends left, we managed to get him calmed down, and the bookstore event turned out to be a big success. Toby seemed to know the entire day was all about him and didn't let his fans down. It was like he was born to be famous.

Between interviews and media appearances, I was also taking a big step in my own career, going through a personal and business coaching process developed by the same Jack Canfield as behind the *Chicken Soup for the Soul* series. I was learning that everyone needed a purpose, and seeing the happiness Toby got from living his purpose—and how this helped him get through the rest of the week—had me wondering what *my* purpose in life really was. I hoped that being coached would point me in the right direction, just as Maggie had done for Toby.

One day, my coach, Gary, asked a question that had me digging deep and discovering some surprising things about myself. "Charmaine," he said, "do you feel you have any tendencies toward perfectionism?"

My brain said *absolutely not*, but I had learned to pause and wait for messages from my body. The question caused my stomach to flip-flop and a warmth to spread through me. *Don't be ridiculous, Charmaine*, my brain said. *If you were a perfectionist, how could you ever put up with Toby?*

"I know I have high standards and worry about making mistakes," I said. "But perfectionism . . . ?"

Gary asked me my definition of perfectionism. "A person who has all the soup cans facing the same way, is a hundred percent orderly, and is what people refer to as 'anal.'"

After I got off the phone, I called my friend Jackie for a second opinion. She had known me for years, and I knew I could count on her to be brutally honest. "Do you think I'm a perfectionist?" I asked. "And why is that such a bad thing, anyway? I don't' get it."

There followed a series of choking noises, followed by loving laughter. "Seriously, Charmaine? Are you telling me that you had no idea you were a perfectionist?"

I received the same sort of responses from Chris and my best friend Rose Anne.

"It's unanimous," I told Toby as I put him on his leash for our walk. "It seems I *am* a perfectionist, and I'm the last one to know. Did *you* know?"

Toby barked once. I laughed and stroked his head. "Oh, you did, did you? Well, why didn't you tell me, you big galoot?"

We headed outside, Toby taking the lead. "I'll tell you one thing," I said to his wagging tail. "From now on, everyone can start referring to me as a recovering perfectionist."

Through the coaching process, I discovered I had created a definition for "perfectionism" I didn't fit into, just so I didn't have to change my perfectionist tendencies. The problem wasn't my love of lists or my appreciation of organization. The problem was that I had difficulty letting things go. I also learned that I subscribed to an all-or-nothing way of looking at life. As I explored these discoveries with Christopher, we realized that he, too, was a perfectionist in his own way and certainly shared my tendency toward all-or-nothing thinking.

Cleaning up one evening after Toby had reorganized our living room yet again, Chris wondered aloud if our extremely helpful, talented superstar of a dog was ever going to stop ripping our home apart. "We've done everything we can think of, and you still do this. What more are we supposed to do?"

Good question. And to me, a thought quickly emerged . . . maybe this was a lesson about acceptance. Perhaps we were meant to come to terms with the fact that Toby wasn't perfect, and while he had improved, he still had issues that we needed to accept. In the middle of our demolished living room, I stopped dead still, a book in each hand.

"What's wrong, Charmaine?"

It took me some time to get my thoughts together. I motioned for Christopher to sit on the couch with me.

"Maybe Toby doesn't *have* to stop tearing the house apart," I said. "Instead, maybe you and I need to let go of our perfectionist ideas of what a dog should be and how a dog should behave. We seem to think the goal is to reach a point where Toby behaves the way we want him to all the time. If he never reaches that point, then we haven't been successful."

Chris shook his head. "We just want him to stop messing up the house when we're away. That's what we've always wanted."

"I think we wanted him to be happier, remember? And we wanted ourselves to be happier. And we've already achieved that."

Christopher was silent, thinking about what I'd said. Slowly, he began to nod. "So you're saying we're engaging in our usual all-or-nothing thinking when it comes to Toby."

"Yes. I think we should just relax and accept that part of loving Toby means accepting a tantrum now and then when we leave him alone. That's just the way it is—and that's okay. Things don't have to be perfect."

"Wow, Char."

"What?"

"I just never thought I'd hear *you* say something doesn't have to be perfect."

I whacked him with a throw pillow. "Look, this is just an idea. I'm not sure if it's right or not. Let's just think about it, okay?"

I could see Christopher's point, for sure. If we just accepted Toby's behavior, it would never change. It was hard to know what the right course of action was. Hopefully the answers would come or Toby would settle down for good.

In the meantime, we just kept serving as entourage for a famous pooch.

Twenty-five

Toby's Playground
Gets Bigger

With Toby being the most famous dog in town, my friend Kaytie, owner of the K9 Awareness Centre, wondered if he would help her out.

"Could Toby be the guest of honor for our grand opening?"

"I think he'd be in his glory. Absolutely. Count us in."

"It would be great if he could do a demonstration on our canine treadmill at the event."

I broke into laughter. Toby on a treadmill? Our dog would go a long way out of his comfort zone when it served his purpose, but I wasn't sure he'd think walking on a scary moving platform was important enough. Still, I told Kaytie she could try.

For its grand opening, the K9 Awareness Centre was

packed with people and dogs. Shortly after the festivities began, Toby made his grand appearance, soaking up the attention and barking to make sure we all knew he was there. *Watch out, world. I have arrived!*

Then came his turn on the treadmill. Chris walked him over to the machine and handed the leash to Kaytie.

"Come on, Toby, up. Good boy." Kaytie guided Toby onto the belt of the treadmill, which was specially designed to be used by dogs. When she turned it on, Toby, clueless as to what to do when the ground started moving under him, simply rolled off the end.

With Kaytie's help, Toby got up again and started walking along the belt. But whenever something captured his attention, he lost his focus and slipped right off the end again. The audience was in tears from laughing.

"Come on, Toby, let's try again," said Kaytie. As a dog trainer, she has the ability to reassure dogs and support them in learning something new. This time Toby refused to take his eyes off the top end of the treadmill, as if staring at it would anchor him to the darn thing. After a few minutes, he actually seemed to be enjoying himself. It was amazing to see how calm and focused he became.

That focus carried through into his television appearance with CTS TV, a program that aired several times and led to invitations for Toby to appear as a special guest at many other events.

So many people wanted to hear about Toby that we decided to get him his own website. A website would allow us to share some of his story and let people send messages to Toby. My parents, proud of their famous granddog, quickly spread the word. The kids at the school where my mom worked were some of the website's first visitors.

It was all happening the way I had dreamt. . . . Toby was making a difference in the world, both in person and on the Internet.

"Just like I said, Toby. You were meant to do big things. Your playground just got much bigger."

Toby was also a sponsor of our neighbors' daughters' soccer team, so we were quick to place a team photo on his website. Actually taking the photo, though, proved to be a laugh and a half. Chris occupied Toby's attention by playing fetch with him while the team members positioned themselves on the field. Then I heard Chris' voice. "Toby, come! Leave it!"

Swinging my head around, I saw Toby drop the Kong from his mouth to give full attention to a rabbit that had run across his path. Toby was off like a shot. The team howled with laughter. Chris called again for Toby—who was on a mission—and he stopped, barked twice, then returned to Chris.

"Toby, where's your Kong?"

Toby took off again, returning moments later with the Kong, just in time for the team photos, with Toby the sponsor in the middle of a group of smiling young teenage girls.

I wanted Toby's website to be an interactive affair, a way for Toby to continue to live his purpose. After some thought, I launched Toby's PAWsitive Inspirations, a weekly positive thought and inspirational message sent from Toby to his followers. A new photo of Toby and a paw print accompanied each message. Now I was living my purpose, too—to inspire others to live their best life, with the help of Toby. Toby's database of followers grew each week.

This was a great project for Chris and me to work on together. "Chris, have you noticed that Toby is actually helping us on this?"

Looking confused, he asked, "How so?"

"Well, remember when we tried to lay the laminate flooring, cut firewood with the chainsaw, paint the house, and even when we began building the garage, we didn't always work so great as a team? And now, working on The Toby Project, we're collaborating and enjoying it."

I left Chris with that thought, as Toby trotted behind me. "You are still our little shadow, Toby, but you know what? It doesn't drive me nuts anymore. In fact, it's a little endearing."

After www.tobytales.com had been running for a while, our niece Ashley suggested that Toby also get on Facebook. I wasn't even on Facebook, but I thought it was a great idea. Facebook would be an easy way for people to follow Toby, and I began to use it to post PAWsitive Inspirations. I kept the messages empowering, enlightening, and inspirational—all the things that Toby himself represented in life. Soon people began to send messages to Toby. It was strange, but enjoyable, to write in Toby's voice. I had to get creative and found the process easy and fun. But the best part was working with Christopher and sharing our excitement over the project. Each week we created PAWsitive Inspirations together and talked about how the message applied to our own lives. The dog who had come between us was bringing us closer together in a powerful way.

Facebook allowed us to connect with a number of other authors who had been featured in *Chicken Soup for the Soul:*

What I Learned from the Dog. I also got in touch with friends I hadn't seen for sixteen years, friends such as Cora, who had introduced me to my husband. We hadn't spoken for fifteen years; not because we'd had a falling out, but because we hadn't put the effort that we should have into our relationship and drifted apart. Now, thanks to Toby, I was attracting people like Cora back into my life, and I vowed that this time I'd work to keep these connections alive.

"Why does Toby attract attention wherever he goes? Why is he so popular?" I asked Christopher, while we were walking to the grocery store one night. "He's such a media magnet. Louise at the bank always comes out to say hello to Toby when you guys walk over with me to do the banking. People always smile at him when we're out on walks. Sometimes, I feel like he's the king of the law of attraction." Snow crunched under our feet, and Toby walked happily beside us. Was it his honest, gentle eyes, his big goofy smile, or his undying curiosity and ability to accept people for who they were? I'd probably never know.

Then Toby stopped walking and started barking madly at something ahead of us. Chris laughed. "It must be his bravery and willingness to protect people that makes him so popular," he said. "Toby, relax. It's a snowman!"

Toby on the Run

Kneeling on the front porch, brushing Toby, I noticed a small patch of gray hair nestled in his dark brown coat. "Gray hairs, Toby?" I asked him. "Don't be getting too old on me, now!" Gray hairs in his reddish-brown coat could only mean one thing: several years had gone by.

Toby put his head on my shoulder and looked into my eyes. He always seemed to know when someone needed a dose of affection.

"Thanks, Toby. I needed that. C'mon, let's get the mail."

When I tore open one envelope, my eyebrows rose. "Toby, this one is actually for you. Looks like you've gotten yourself invited to participate in Words in the Park."

This was exciting. Words in the Park is an event for local authors—and in our case, their four-legged subjects.

It is called "Words in the Park" because the event takes place in our community, Sherwood Park, although it is held in the library. I wasn't concerned about that; Toby had had plenty of practice at book signings now, so this would be a breeze.

On the day of the event, Toby and I headed to the library with my niece Ashley, who had taken take time off from her university classes to give me a hand setting up. We were expecting a big turnout. The event had enjoyed lots of publicity, with Toby gracing a poster and other marketing material.

"Thanks for coming today, Ash," I murmured as we walked an excited Toby into the building.

Ashley looked around uncertainly. "Toby is awfully full of energy. I'm guessing this is his first time in a library." Toby walked proudly, tail wagging and tongue bouncing in and out of his mouth as he pranced ahead of us, sniffing everything within reach. People peered curiously around the stacks.

One of the librarians approached. "This must be Toby," she said with a smile. "Hi, Toby! It is great to have you here. This is the first time we've had a dog at the event." Toby barked twice. *My pleasure!*

As the librarian directed us to our table, stopping to greet other people along the way, I whispered to Ashley, "I hope that's not our table. There's a guinea pig in a cage on it. Toby will go nuts." I could just picture him scrambling gleefully through the library after a terrified rodent. Bending down, I whispered, "Okay, Toby, it's best behavior time. You're a good boy."

"Here we are," the librarian said. "You can share this

table with our other four-legged guest of honor." Ashley and I exchanged worried looks, but Toby was too busy taking in everything else to notice the guinea pig.

We began setting up our display table, laying out copies of *Chicken Soup for the Soul*, Toby's bookmarks and magnets, and some Chimo Project–related material. As I reached into my bag, Toby's Kong toy fell out and rolled onto the carpet. Ashley tried to grab it, but Toby was there first, snatching it up and tossing it to one of the guests, then barking wildly. Despite my efforts, he would not settle down; he wanted someone to toss him the Kong. He wanted to play, and I could not get him to recognize that this was *not* a play zone. People were looking up from their tables and a few children clung to their parents, startled by Toby's bark.

"I'll take the Kong out to the car," said Ashley. "Distract him for a minute."

"There is no distracting him from the Kong," I said. But I spoke too soon. Toby had just spotted the guinea pig, now in a little girl's arms. While we were organizing the table, the owner had let children hold the famous guinea pig.

Before I could act, Toby lunged forward to check out this living stuffed animal. Thankfully, I pulled the leash in at the same time the rodent owner scooped the guinea pig out of the little girl's arms. There was a resounding "Ohhhhhhh" from the crowd as Toby pulled up short. Stuffing the Kong into her bag, Ashley escorted Toby outside to see if some fresh air would help him settle.

When they returned ten minutes later, I had the booth organized and could focus on helping Toby enjoy the day.

In no time, children and their parents surrounded us.

Toby stopped fidgeting and forgot about the guinea pig. He was eager to visit with the kids.

"Can I pet him?" asked a girl of perhaps six.

"Sure." I showed her the correct way to approach Toby. "What's your name?"

"Jenny."

"Toby, say hello to Jenny."

Toby barked and licked Jenny's hand. Delighted, she gave him a few gentle pats.

"I can't have a dog because my mom has allergies," she said. "And I really, really want one."

"Maybe you can have one when you grow up."

Her eyes lit up. "I'm going to. And it's going to be just like Toby."

The children took turns petting Toby. He was friendly and gentle, and visiting with them gave him something to focus on, calming him down. Thank goodness. I had been worried that we were not going to be able to participate in the event, but now, trusting that Toby would stay seated and behave himself, I eased my death grip on his leash.

That was when Jenny's father called her away from the group. As she turned to leave, Toby spotted a stuffed bear peeking from her backpack. In Toby's experience, all stuffed animals had been created for his enjoyment. He barked and scrambled to his feet so fast the leash jerked from my hand. I made a dive for it, but Toby was already off after Jenny, who had spun around at his bark—making the stuffed animal fall to the floor.

"Toby!" I cried. "Sit! Toby! Leave it!"

I might as well have been ordering a stone to grow legs and walk. With single-minded determinedness, Toby picked up the bear and disappeared between two high rows of shelving, likely to play with his new furry friend.

"Toby! Come!"

Jenny's face tightened. "Toby took Gingerbear, Daddy!"

Her father assured her she'd get her bear back while giving me a dubious look. The crowd of kids and parents were all talking excitedly. I wished that Ashley hadn't left for work already, because between the two of us we could trap Toby in an aisle. On my own, I was helpless. Toby wasn't in the row I'd seen him enter. Nor in either of the rows flanking it.

"Toby! Come! I have a treat for you. Toby!" I felt terrible talking that loud in a library. I just hoped Toby wouldn't decide to mark his territory.

"There he is!" A boy pointed toward the far end of the library, by the guinea pig. Toby, the stuffed bear clamped firmly in his mouth, had gone back to our table to await my return.

"I have to get to him before he does any damage," I said out loud, but mostly to myself. Toby's behavior reminded me of the day he took off full speed ahead after a jackrabbit in the park. Chris and I had never seen Toby run that fast, and it was the first time he had ever been out of our eyesight. The experience must have scared him, too, because when he came back he was elated to see us.

Jenny and her dad were also making their way over to our table. I reached Toby just as he dropped the bear at Jenny's feet and began licking her hand. He knew that returning the bear would make Jenny feel better. And, of course, it worked. Jenny wrapped her arms around his neck.

"Good boy, Toby. You brought my bear back. Good boy."

Toby looked very pleased with himself, but I was tempted to scold him. Once again, a stuffed animal dropped at someone's feet had been the offering for forgiveness. Gripping his leash and gritting my teeth, I gave him the "look," but reminded myself there was no point in getting angry with him. I was the one who had released my grip on the leash, and I was the one who had taught Toby that stuffed animals were all meant for him. Toby was smart, but I couldn't expect a dog to understand the rules of libraries. "Oh, Toby. You are going to be the end of me, I swear." I collapsed in a chair. He sat at my feet, smiling at the slowly dispersing crowd.

After that, Toby was good for the rest of the event. There were several speeches and poetry readings. Toby sat quietly watching the speakers and readers until the very end, and then, barked loudly when the speeches were completed. *Finally. Let's get back to visiting.*

The experts said he had a vocabulary of two hundred. I think it was more like two thousand.

Twenty-seven

Terror in the Park

It was a beautiful day, the sky a brilliant October blue, a perfect backdrop for the yellow leaves that top the trees in our part of the world.

Toby seemed to know we were driving to the off-leash park from the moment we left the house. "Enough, Toby," I said, when I couldn't take his barking anymore. Always insistent on having the last word, he barked once more, then settled for giving out the occasional whine. He sounded like a child asking that inevitable question: *Are we there yet?*

As we made the last turn on the road to the park, Toby began to ready himself to jump out of the truck. Sure enough, when we stopped, he burst from the truck as if he had been cooped up forever. He ran in circles, barked uncontrollably, leapt into the air. *We're here! We're here!*

Christopher and I also enjoyed the off-leash park, located in a beautiful part of the city with wooded trails always packed with families and their dogs. We liked meeting other dog lovers and watching Toby play and socialize with other dogs. Truth be told, we also loved seeing the shenanigans that went on in the park. Watching the dogs was as fun as watching a group of children playing in the sandbox together. We got a kick out of seeing Toby and the other dogs running to their owners to tattle when another dog had taken their toys.

"Looks like he's happy to be here," said Christopher as we got out of the truck, and Toby—without warning or permission—bounded off to greet the other dogs. I knew his real intention was to investigate who had sticks, balls, Frisbees, or Kongs to chase. After thoroughly checking the truck for his Kong and Frisbee, we realized we had accidentally left his fetching toys at home.

Adapting to the situation, Toby ran into the bushes in search of a stick.

Christopher and I burst into laughter when we saw him struggling to get out of the bushes with his find—a log six feet long and several inches in diameter. Dropping it and barking with pride and excitement, Toby challenged anyone close by to throw the log for him.

There were no takers.

Christopher eventually distracted Toby from the log and walked into the bushes to find a more reasonably sized branch. He returned with a big stick, thick but not sharp on either end—the perfect fetching stick.

"Toby, get it!" Chris threw the stick, and off Toby ran.

A boxer and a cream-colored Labradoodle wanted in on the action and chased Toby as Toby chased the stick. At one point, the Labradoodle and Toby each held onto an end of the stick. As they ran alongside each other, we laughed with the other dog's owners. There had been a time when Toby hadn't been able to handle other dogs taking hold of his stick. It used to make him nervous, and he would run back to us, barking, complaining in his own way that somebody had unfairly taken his toy, and he wanted it back. But over time, he'd gotten into the game and was now happy to share, running until the other dog dropped the stick, then taking off quickly, partly to escape the other dog and partly to encourage the other dog to chase him.

Distracted by a passing dog, the Labradoodle dropped the stick, and Toby brought it to us for another game of fetch, barking loudly. *Come on, Chris, hurry up! Throw it!*

Christopher picked up the stick and ordered Toby to circle. Toby orbited Christopher twice. On the third time around, Christopher hurled the stick. It lodged in the ground and Toby charged up to it, mouth yawning, and snatched it up.

Then he stopped, looking startled, and yelped loudly. He dropped the stick. We knew instantly that something was wrong and hurried over to him. Toby's eyes looked panicked. When I saw blood, my knees went weak.

"Oh, Christopher, he's bleeding and it looks bad. It looks as though the stick jabbed in his throat."

"It's okay boy. Open your mouth, Toby. Let's have a look," Christopher prodded. It took some doing, but eventually Toby opened his mouth.

"I can't see anything cut, and can't tell where the blood

is coming from. It looks like it's slowing down. What should we do?" I asked.

We decided to stay and to observe Toby, so we'd know if we should be heading to a vet's office.

As we continued to monitor Toby, we saw that he didn't want to lie down, but did sit between us. He seemed distracted by the dogs chasing Frisbees and balls, and after about ten minutes, started looking and acting as if he was fine. The bleeding stopped, and he went chasing after a ball thrown to another dog, tail wagging and tongue flopping in and out of his mouth.

Relieved, I leaned over, hands on my knees, trying to slow my rapidly pounding heart. "I think we better go," I said. "This is enough excitement for one day."

On the drive home, Toby was quiet, but that was typical after a good game of chase and fetch. Once home, however, he remained unusually subdued. He left the television room, where Chris and I were watching a movie, and I found him in the downstairs washroom, lying on the green mat. I called Chris. "Something about Toby just isn't right."

"Why don't you phone Erin? She used to work for a vet."

Toby just watched us, his head on one paw, looking a little forlorn.

After calling Erin, I returned to the washroom and told Christopher help was on the way. Within minutes, the doorbell rang. Toby did not bark or move. That removed all doubt that something was seriously wrong. At any other time, seeing him lie still while someone was at the door would have been a dream come true. Now it was devastating.

Erin gave Toby a quick examination and looked worried. "He's started drooling, and he's too quiet. It seems like he might be in shock."

Chris and I exchanged anxious glances. "What should we do?" I asked.

"You can either wait a bit and see what happens, or take him to the emergency clinic. If he doesn't improve soon, definitely get him to the clinic."

Watching Toby closely after Erin left, I knew we shouldn't wait.

"Chris, I'm going to take him to the clinic. I know it's late, and it will cost, but he's not right. I'll take him; I know you have to be up early tomorrow."

Christopher helped me put Toby in the truck. The half-hour drive to the clinic seemed to take much longer than usual, the silence from the backseat was almost unbearable. Toby made no attempts to sneak into the front seat, and I missed the comforting weight of his head on my shoulder.

In the clinic, Toby did not show any interest in the rabbit, cat, or two other dogs in the waiting room. He just sat facing me with his head on my lap, looking at me with his big, beautiful brown and yellow eyes. I felt helpless. "Toby, I'd like to explain how you're about to endure some unpleasant testing, but it's for your own good, okay?" He just looked at me. All I could do was what Toby did for me when I was upset or hurting—sit with him, fully present in the moment, and look lovingly into his eyes.

As we waited for our turn with the vet, I reflected on the number of accidents and close calls Toby had had over the years. He'd been skunked at the lake cottage, racing out of the woods stinking more than I ever imagined possible. It was unbearable. Even Toby turned his nose up at himself as we walked back along the gravel road to our cottage. We had to keep him outside on the porch that night, pure torture for our social animal. Toby couldn't understand why he was suddenly the victim of such harsh and unfair treatment, and his barking and whining nearly drove us crazy. He finally fell asleep after tiring himself out. We awoke to toenails clicking on the sliding door and the smell of skunk.

He'd also become severely dehydrated one summer weekend after too much fun under the sun at the cottage. That had resulted in Chris and me waiting patiently for an hour while the vet injected two IV bags into Toby, plumping him up with liquid until he resembled a grizzly bear. Then there was the jackrabbit incident, in which Toby had miraculously dodged traffic as he chased in full-on pursuit a rabbit on a busy city street.

One drama after another. But he always survived. I tried to reassure myself that this time would be no different.

Earlier that week, I had experienced two close calls. In the first one I had driven the Blazer home, aware that the handling was off but unable to find anything amiss when I pulled over and checked the vehicle. But when I turned into the driveway, I saw Christopher waving both arms and yelling at me to stop: one of the wheels was almost off, wobbling like crazy as I drove. Chris discovered that the wheel was held on by only a single bolt. It could easily have flown off on the highway, causing a serious accident.

As Chris examined the wheel, I looked up and was shocked to see a car in my flower garden. I asked Chris what was going on. It turned out that the little boy across the street had been playing in his dad's car and put it into reverse. It rolled down their driveway, across the street, and into our garden. "Luckily he didn't hit the tree or Toby," Christopher pointed out.

That boy and I had both been watched over by our guardian angels. I could only pray that Toby's angel would watch out for him, too.

Twenty-eight

Love and Loss

"At first glance," the vet said, "it looks like Toby has two large lacerations in his throat. One is about the size of a dollar coin. He might need surgery; the surgeon who is on in the morning will evaluate that. I also found foreign material, probably fragments of the stick, that will have to be removed from his throat and mouth first to prevent complication and infection. So we'll need to sedate him, put him on an IV, and see how he gets through the night. Why don't I prepare you an estimate of what the costs will be so you can make some decisions about what you want to do?"

My stomach flopped. "Preparing an estimate" meant this would be a costly procedure and thus a serious one. I agreed to look at the estimate but knew I didn't need to see it. Whatever the cost, forgoing medical treatment for

Toby was not an option. We had come too far together. He was part of our family.

Toby lay quietly on the examination table while I phoned Chris. He answered on the first ring, and I explained what the vet had said. "I'll call you back when the vet brings in the estimate and tells me how we should proceed."

"How are you doing?" Chris asked. I could only cry. Toby looked over, and in his eyes, I saw his constant desire to make things right. At that moment, messes in the hallway and broken toilet tank lids became inconsequential.

When the vet returned, his face was grim. "This looks pretty serious. I'm pretty sure Toby will need surgery, and my best estimate is that it will cost between $1,800 and $2,600. Depending on what the surgeon says in the morning, we might have to transfer Toby to Western Veterinary Clinic or to Calgary to operate."

Gasping back sobs, I eventually caught my breath and told him I needed to call my husband. "Chris, are you sitting down? That damn stick has caused between $1,800 and $2,600 of damage. It's pretty serious."

"What do you think? What should we do?"

"I want to fix him up. We just have to. You should see him. He is not okay. He seems . . . lifeless."

Chris supported the decision to do whatever was required to make Toby better. Here we were, I thought, ready to spend a small fortune to save a dog that we had almost given away not so long ago.

Gently, I hugged Toby good-bye. He didn't even try to get up or come with me.

Crying all the way home, I prayed that Toby would make it through the night; that the same angel who had watched over Chris and me in the lake twelve years earlier and who had protected me in the truck earlier that week, would watch over Toby through the hours to come.

When I got home, Christopher was sitting up in bed, the lamp on and a book in his lap.

"You have to work in the morning," I said. "What are you doing up?"

"There's no way I can sleep. How is he? How are you?"

"Not good." Fresh tears began to flow, and I fought to keep from sobbing like a child. Christopher pulled me into his arms.

"It's okay, sweetheart. Let's just hope for the best."

I cried on his shoulder for a while as he stroked my hair. I was reminded of the day Dooks died, a day that was both terrible and sweet thanks to the memory of a young man I'd run into just days before.

I'd just left my office on a sandwich run and was hurrying down the street, eager to get out of the cold, when I heard someone say hello. Looking up, I saw a young man, around the age of twenty-one, smiling at me. It took only seconds before I realized who he was, in spite of the fact that he'd changed considerably in the eleven years since I'd last seen him at the drop-in youth center that I had operated at the time.

"Derrick!" I hugged him. "You're all grown up. I can't believe this!"

"I was actually on my way to see you at your office but heard you'd moved." He smiled at my shocked expression. "I just wanted to let you know my life turned out okay. I'm doing good!"

Time seemed to stop. As a boy, Derrick had whittled his way into both Christopher's heart and mine, and we had often wondered what had happened to him.

"Derrick, you have no idea how wonderful it is to see you. Thank you for taking the time to find me."

"Do you still have Dooks?"

I told him we did, but that Dooks was quite old and his health was failing.

"Dooks really helped me that day when I couldn't go home because of the abuse," he said. "Remember?"

I did. I hoped Derrick would think it was the wind that made my eyes water.

"Chris brought Dooks to the drop-in center," he said. "I didn't want to talk to anybody. I didn't know what to say. Families aren't supposed to be like mine, you know?"

I nodded. Oh, how I knew. I remembered that day, and how, helping him, I had felt like a mother. Standing up for a child, his rights, his safety, and his future, because no one else spoke on his behalf.

"But Dooks kept me company," he said, "and I even told him a few things because I knew he wasn't going to tell anyone else. You gave me a picture of him, the one you had in your office, when I left with the social workers, remember? I kept it for a long time."

A few days later, Dooks died. I was in the house when Chris called for me to come outside. Dooks lay in the grass, his brown eyes vacant. He was still breathing, but clearly not for much longer. I sat on the grass, gathered him in my arms and held him as his breathing gradually slowed and finally stopped. The entire world seemed to have stopped; everything was still and quiet.

Christopher held me then, just as he held me now as Toby fought for his life in a clinic half a city away from us and I cried my heart out—for Dooks, for us, for a little boy so hurt he could trust no one but a big white dog.

Suddenly, an anger I had been unwilling to admit to feeling burst from me. "Why did we even get Toby? Why did we keep him? Jeez! Christopher, we were just fine without him!"

"Honey, what are you talking about? You love Toby."

"But I wouldn't, if we hadn't decided to get another dog. I wouldn't even know him. I wouldn't . . ." I was so sad, so afraid, so wounded by my love for Toby.

That was the thing, I thought to myself. The thing to remember in all of this: it was about love. Would I really give back all the love Toby had given me, Christopher, the patients at the hospital? A second before, gripped by fear, I would have said yes. But with just a little distance, I knew that every moment with Toby had been worth this suffering and the greater suffering that would, inevitably, follow.

It was a long night. Surprisingly, I fell asleep at some point. The phone woke me the next morning. I snatched it up before it had made a full ring, with sleep fogging my mind and blinding sunlight pouring in the bedroom window.

I immediately recognized the voice of the vet I'd spoken to the night before. "Toby made it through the night okay, Charmaine. The good news is that his blood results are okay. We were able to safely remove the remnants of the stick and, so far, no infection."

My heart soared. Then plunged.

"The bad news is that the lacerations are so severe we can't close them. If we try, the likelihood of them opening again and causing further damage is very high. We want to see how Toby's wounds heal naturally over the next ten to fourteen days, then try the surgery; that should increase the chances of success."

Twenty-nine

A Lesson in Faith

I picked up Toby as soon as the emergency clinic allowed. The vet told me what to expect. "His breathing will sound bubbly or gurgly because he's breathing in and out through the wound. If you notice any bleeding, take him to your vet right away. We'll call Dr. Lyons's office to advise her of our intended plan of action.

"If you notice any food coming from his nose, call us or your vet immediately. Any diarrhea, lethargy, or loss of appetite—call immediately. He can't eat anything that's hard or requires chewing. Just give him soft food for two weeks."

Looking at Toby, I felt swamped with shame. How could we have let this happen? Why had we done something so stupid? But the vet explained that this type of injury is common; he had seen it many times. Usually it was caused when a dog ran with a stick in its mouth and the stick suddenly jammed into the ground, tearing a hole in the dog's mouth or throat.

We'd had no idea that playing fetch with sticks was so dangerous. I made a mental note to educate the other dog owners in the park as soon as we got back there.

At home, I made Toby comfortable on the floor in my office where I could keep a close eye on him. Each gurgling breath tore at me. What would we do without him? I couldn't bear the thought. "You okay, buddy?"

Toby looked at me mournfully.

"You just rest, okay? I'll be right here."

I shuddered to think of how his patients would feel if Toby stopped coming to visit. And what about his fans, the many people who followed his story through Facebook, visited his website, and kept in touch? This dog had a circle of friends larger than that of many humans. Losing Toby would affect many lives.

Thinking of Toby's fans, I was reminded of a story I'd received from a woman in California. Giuliana had become a dog walker by chance after her divorce and had quickly discovered she had a talent for understanding dogs and helping them improve their behavior. Her words resonated with me now:

> It is not easy to adopt a pet. They become part of your life and you have to be ready to sacrifice your time and love and attention, and a million other things! It is a dog's lifetime of serious work. The few that are really ready for the above are honest-to-God, real pet

lovers and, most likely, have been trained by a previous pet. The rest are just rookies.

Giuliana wrote stories about the dogs she worked with, stories that presented the dogs as characters in their own right. That evening, while Christopher and I listened to Toby's labored breathing, I pulled one out.

"Chris, I want to share this story with you. The author really understands dogs, and the story gives me hope that Toby will make it through this challenge."

Shar Pei
by Giuliana Temme

One afternoon I was called with what turned out to be the most intriguing job offer I ever received. The summons came from one of the biggest wine makers of Napa Valley. His story was, as he put it, mystifying.

Several days before, a beautiful cream-colored Shar Pei simply walked into the winery office and sat in front of this man's desk. Various attempts were made to evict the stray, all at no avail. The dog kept evading the evictors, always returning to the man's side, staring at that gentleman with adoring eyes. I suspect he read the man well and understood his vanity; however, I also believe he had a nose for money! The Shar Pei would not let anyone touch him but this gentleman. It was as if the Shar Pei was saying, "Come on, look at me! I am so beautiful and I love you! Here, I'll prove it—let me lick your hand. Please adopt me!"

Of course, the most wonderful experience in life is to feel loved, wanted, and even adored. The gentleman in question melted like ice on a hot sidewalk. The dog won. Where the man went, the dog followed. They were inseparable, except for about twenty minutes each and every day.

Those twenty minutes became a haunting question for the man because, other than during those minutes, the dog was at his side constantly. When it was time for bed, the dog competed with the man's wife for the last kiss good night and, in the morning, for the first smile. At lunch, he was there for a morsel of food, but in the early afternoon the dog was gone. He simply disappeared every day for about twenty minutes. The man tried to follow the dog, even posting winery employees in strategic positions trying to get a clue as to its whereabouts, but with no luck. No one could follow or even catch a glimpse of the Shar Pei during those twenty minutes.

My word-of-mouth reputation as a self-made dog shrink impressed the winery owner and he felt it gave me the necessary credentials to undertake this mystery job. It turned out his wife was a psychiatrist. She and I had a very long talk about the Shar Pei, who sat behind the winery owner's chair during the entire conversation, eyeing me in a composed, calm manner. "We did everything in our power to find his original owner," said the man's wife. "All with no results. The dog had no tag or any other means of identification. By the time the investigating was done, my husband had already fallen head over heels in love with him. We decided to adopt him and simply call him Shar Pei.

"He fits into our lifestyle. We own this winery so he has plenty of space. But he is puzzling us. He loves my husband and never leaves his side, except for those twenty minutes every day. We are not concerned about losing him because he always comes back but we would like to have an answer to this mystery. In short, we want to know the reason for his disappearance."

Shar Pei eyed her and yawned. It made me laugh. Giving him a sly side-glance, I assured the couple I would do everything in my power to solve this great mystery. After I made that promise I looked at the dog again and this time I laughed out loud! The look on his face said, "Oh yeah right, Toots!"

The assignment started when I took Shar Pei to my Napa Valley barn. He did not like to be touched or caressed and, in fact, he avoided any physical contact whatsoever. I respected his wishes and followed his rules. He willingly jumped in the car with the other critters in my care, but kept himself aloof. When they went out to run, he always ran alone, following the other dogs' games from some distance. He started his disappearing act the very first day.

My walking system differs from those of other dog walkers. I don't believe in the leash unless used for training purposes. Discharging physical energy requires space so, even on my Napa Valley patch of land, I always drove out to open fields and let them have the full taste of freedom, all dogs totally off leash, running and playing until they exhausted themselves.

Shar Pei did his disappearing act regularly for that first week and I did not attempt to stop him. When he came back from wherever he had been, he would eye me to see if any reaction could be detected. Once assured there was none, he'd begin to mingle with the others, always making sure no physical contact occurred. The other dogs didn't care and didn't seem to like him very much. When games were played, I was his partner most of the time.

A week passed before I made my move. In the meantime, I began to talk about this mystery with other dog walkers at the play area, and also with local dog owners at their favorite hangout. Except for a few jokes, nobody seemed to have a clue.

I took Shar Pei into the city with me, walking him around on a leash. Everyone loved him; he just had a special way about him. But he found a way to escape for twenty minutes, leaving me heart attack prone, waiting for him to return. He came back, leash dangling and, on his beautiful face, a sorrowful but guilty look.

One day I finally made my move. I drove to a place where the bushes were sparse and I could see him for miles. I had with me a pair of binoculars and a bike. After a few minutes of frolicking he took off. I gave him some distance and then jumped on the bike and followed him. Suddenly he stopped and looked behind him. I managed to flatten myself and the bike to the ground, grabbed the binoculars and fastened my sights on him. He evidently felt assured no one was near him and suddenly began to vomit for what must have been ten minutes straight. I could see that it was a strange orange color. He sat looking at it, and then the sequence repeated itself as he relieved his body of that strange substance. When he was finished, he started back toward the play area, but before then I was already pedaling to the car.

I called the lady from my car the moment I dropped Shar Pei at his home. As soon as she answered I began to tell her what happened. "I believe Shar Pei is a very sick dog. I do not know the nature of his sickness but I know he is sick. I also don't know how he manages to hide it all day until he is alone, but my advice is to take him to a good vet immediately."

The lady took Shar Pei to the vet but nothing was found. The dog, according to the vet, was "fit as a fiddle."

I suffered the laughter and teasing of friends and the doubtful looks of Shar Pei's owners about my so-called "dog-shrink" capabilities, but I continued to believe in my diagnosis.

The more time passed, the more I was convinced the dog was very sick and extremely adept at hiding his problem. Sadly, the day finally came when the Shar Pei could no longer hide his sickness. On that day his owners gathered him up and took him to a vet in New York, a renowned specialist. The results were astonishing and far more severe than I had guessed.

Shar Pei had a very rare illness, most likely caused from eating diseased, wild rabbit. His body was slowly digesting itself. On top of that, he also had a 22-caliber bullet lodged one inch from his liver. That told us the whole story of how Shar Pei had come to be separated from his original owner.

Somewhere in a field in Napa Valley his heartless owner, who was obviously aware of his sickness, had shot him and left him for dead. Shar Pei learned a hard lesson that day: never show your sickness. I believe he healed himself from the bullet wound through sheer will power and found a new owner, making sure nobody discovered his secret, until he could no longer hide it.

Shar Pei never came back from New York. On the day I returned his leash and things, I found a letter waiting for me, a beautiful letter. Tears flowed from my eyes as I read the comforting words. They still do every time I think of him. My friends sent me a beautiful bouquet called Spring Time for Shar Pei—and life went on. I am so glad he had wonderful people that cared and loved him at the end.

Christopher hugged me as I put the story down. "If anyone has the strength to heal himself, it's Toby. We had faith that he would settle down one day, and he has gotten a lot better. We need to have faith that he can beat this, too."

I knew he was right, and Giuliana's story bolstered my faith. But I didn't know if faith would be enough.

Thirty

Not Again!

Toby healed slowly. Christopher and I healed even more slowly. We were wracked with guilt over what had happened.

After the first week, the gurgles and burbles from Toby's throat lessened. A good sign. He still slept much of the time and didn't show much interest in food. Because he wasn't interested in playing, I took to brushing him a couple of times a day. It gave him a nice massage and allowed us to spend time together.

"There. You're gorgeous. World's most handsome dog." I set the brush aside and kissed his muzzle. Toby nuzzled me back and half-heartedly licked my cheek.

"It's nice to know you forgive me, buddy." Toby stood up, shook himself, and smiled a big toothy grin. *I disagree.* He was definitely feeling better.

After two weeks, we took him to Dr. Lyons. If Toby's wounds were healing, he would be scheduled for surgery. Another hurdle for us to get over. If they weren't healing . . . I didn't know what would happen, and I tried hard not to think about it.

"So, Toby, you've gotten yourself into a bit of a pickle, have you?" Dr. Lyons had been brought up to date by the staff at the emergency clinic. "Let's see if you're ready for surgery. Open wide." Reluctantly, Toby allowed the vet to examine him.

"This is wonderful. The wounds have healed nicely. I don't think he's going to need surgery."

"Did you hear that, Toby? You're amazing!" I wrapped my arms around my dog, who was now licking my face with vigor. He seemed to understand that the danger had passed, and hurried into the reception area to get a special treat to celebrate the occasion.

Dr. Lyons walked me out. "Keep him on soft food for another few days. Oh, and just so you know, I've begun telling all my dogs' owners to avoid playing fetch with sticks."

"That's great. The vet at the clinic mentioned that this kind of injury happens a lot, but I'd never heard of it."

"No, we don't tend to advise people about it, but we need to start. The truth is that Toby could have died from this injury if you'd left it too long and he'd developed an infection or if the wounds hadn't healed. And what a shame that would have been. All because of a stick."

I told the vet about my guilt over the incident. She placed her hand on my arm. "Accidents happen, and of course we feel bad about our roles in them. The best thing to do is to talk about what happened to Toby, and maybe that will prevent another dog from experiencing the same fate."

Toby's recovery was nothing short of a miracle, and a lot of good luck. Christopher and I did not take either for granted. We reflected long and hard on the adventures our incorrigible dog had taken us on since the day we'd adopted him. We had gone from loving Toby to almost surrendering him to being unable to imagine life without him. A million minor crises had made us question, again and again, our decision to keep him. Then this single big crisis had made every other challenge seem miniscule, and one thing had finally become absolutely certain: Toby was home to stay.

At the dog park, he greeted his old friends with excitement. Christopher and I took every opportunity to tell other dog owners about our close call. When we saw someone innocently tossing a stick, we took the time to stop and explain the dangers. Our goal was, and continues to be, to prevent other dogs from being hurt or even killed in this way. The people we spoke with were always grateful and vowed to stop using sticks in their games.

It's just one more way Toby has touched the lives of others.

Life became so normal again that I was only half listening to Christopher as he described Toby's antics one day. Focused on organizing my wallet, I mumbled, "Where did you say you found Toby?"

"Sitting in the downstairs bathroom sink."

That got my attention. The bathroom sink? I could not picture our enormous mutt wedging himself into a tiny sink.

Christopher explained what had happened. "I couldn't find Toby, so I checked every room in the house. When I got downstairs, the bathroom door was closed, and as soon as I opened it I could smell dog. I figured he'd be right at the door waiting for me to open it, but when I called his name I heard his collar jingle to my left. So I flipped on the light, and no kidding . . . there was Toby, sitting in the sink."

"That's hilarious. No one will ever believe that."

I honestly thought Christopher was kidding until about a week later, when Ashley came home and gave me another odd report. "You'll never guess where Toby was today: sitting in the bathroom sink."

I turned to Toby, who was lying in a spot of sunlight, chewing on a bone. "You're getting weirder every day, mister."

Life with Toby had always had its surprises and mysteries, but this twist was a real winner. What could possibly possess a ninety-pound retriever to haul his butt up on a small counter in order to sit in a little sink?

It was funny until several bad-boy incidents occurred in the space of a week; then I started to worry. Toby's misbehavior had become so much less frequent than it had once been; the sudden rash of closet emptying and bookshelf disasters seemed out of place. He had even chewed three of our shelves.

"Something must be wrong with Toby, Christopher. He's never purposefully chewed our furniture before. That seems out of character, even for him. I think I'll make a vet appointment and get it checked out."

Although Chris chalked up the incidents to "Toby being Toby," he let me have my way.

The day before we were to see the vet, we were playing fetch when Toby started to limp and tripped over his own foot. He actually took a couple of time-outs and chose not to run after the ball. I knew he had to be in pain if he didn't want to chase a ball. Something was wrong with his leg. Calling it a day, Toby and I headed home. I massaged his leg and kept him still to help it heal. I was glad I had a vet appointment booked.

At the clinic, Toby was out of sorts. Although he was normally well behaved at the vet, on this day he was unruly. He climbed up on me while we waited and tried to twist behind me, as if to hide. Next he tried climbing the wall, scratching me in the process.

"Toby! Down. What is up with you? You like Dr. Lyons. She always gives you a massage, remember?"

The door opened. "Toby, what's up?" As Dr. Lyons checked Toby over, I noticed that she was inspecting one side in particular. She looked through Toby's chart and then resumed checking his side. "Toby has a few new lumps," she said. For a long time, Toby had had two large, noncancerous cysts on his side. They were about the size of mandarin oranges, and I called them his "fat sacks." But the new lumps were different.

"Given the change in his behavior, loss of appetite, and injured leg, I'd like to do a more thorough assessment and check out these lumps. We want to be able to rule out cancer."

I gasped. "Cancer?"

"I count eleven new lumps since his last checkup six months ago. We just want to rule out whatever we can so we can get Toby well."

Once again, I would have to leave Toby at the vet's office. After all we'd been through recently, now we had to deal with cancer? I couldn't even get my mind around what was going on.

I held Toby's head in my hands and touched my nose to his. "You're going to stay with the doctor for a little while. I'll come back, okay? And when I do, the doctor is going to tell us that you are absolutely fine. Got it?"

Toby's wagged his tail and licked my nose. Thank goodness he can't understand what's really going on, I thought.

Later that afternoon, Dr. Lyons called. "We've run a number of tests and need to examine the lumps further because the cellular formation indicates a possibility of cancer. We should know the results tomorrow."

In the meantime, she said, we could bring Toby back home. "He might be quiet and lethargic, as he's been poked and prodded quite a bit with the tests, and he's pretty sore."

I called Christopher; he was silent when I shared the news.

Thirty-one

Old Bones

When I picked up Toby the next day, Dr. Lyons took me aside and showed me the X-rays of his sore leg. "Whatever else is going on, Toby also has severe arthritis; he's lost a great deal of muscle mass in his leg. It's amazing he hasn't been acting up more. He must be in a great deal of pain."

"What can we do about the arthritis?"

"Well, it can't be reversed, but we can do a series of injections, one each week for four weeks, and also provide some medication to help rebuild and strengthen cartilage. Unfortunately, this is what life with Toby will be like now. He'll have good days and not-so-good days. But at least with the medication, we'll be able to keep him comfortable and out of pain." She stroked Toby. "This little trooper has such a high threshold for pain, he doesn't let you know when he's hurting."

That night was a sad one at our house. Christopher and I didn't talk about the possibility of cancer, focusing instead on the devil that did have a name: arthritis. We took turns massaging Toby's leg and spoiled him with his favorite soft dog food. After researching arthritis in dogs on the Internet, we decided that we could handle the situation and would do our best to keep Toby active and vibrant for a long time to come. We tried to be positive, but every time the word *cancer* niggled its way into my brain—which it did about four billion times that evening—worms of fear scrambled across the bottom of my stomach.

The next day, Christopher and I held hands while I called Dr. Lyons's office. At her first words, I burst into tears, terrifying Chris. Seeing the look on his face, I almost dropped the phone.

"Oh no, Chris! No! He's okay. It's not cancer!"

We held each other for a long time, then hurried to get Toby's arthritis medication into him.

Toby had had his first injection the day Dr. Lyons diagnosed his arthritis. The following week, when we went back for injection number two, Toby put on the brakes as he reached the door.

"Come on, Toby. You're a good boy! Come on." I tugged at him, but when a Chesapeake Bay retriever doesn't want to move, he isn't going to move. I held out one of his favorite treats and did my best to calm him down. Finally, the vet's assistant stepped in.

"Maybe we'll just do the shot out here, as he's pretty anxious. He likely remembers all the needles and poking and prodding we did last week."

Another assistant and I held Toby firmly, and the shot

was almost finished when Toby squirmed and broke the needle. I felt terrible that I was forcing him to go through this ordeal.

The assistant managed to complete the injection on the second attempt. Toby couldn't wait to leave. I hoped he'd forget about the needles by the following week.

No such luck. The minute we got inside the vet clinic on week three, Toby turned and managed to get the heavy glass door open and escape into the parking lot. I caught up to him and put him on the leash again, and back we went to get the dirty deed accomplished. "I'm sorry, Toby, but we have to do this. You can have a treat after."

But treats were no consolation. After that Toby was absolutely petrified of the vet's clinic, frantically trying to escape on every visit.

"I suppose dogs are just like us that way," I said to Christopher. "A bad experience is etched in your mind, and you become nervous and anxious in similar circumstances. I'll bet he chewed those shelves last week because he was in pain. He was giving us all kinds of clues—the closet, the bookshelves, the sink, chewing stuff. We just didn't understand."

The arthritis treatment and medication seemed to make a difference, although we noticed that Toby's leg still caused him discomfort on very cold days. We had to crush up his glucosamine pills because he always found them if we hid them intact in dog food or wrapped in cheese. The process brought back memories of my mom and dad crushing up my aspirin and mixing it with strawberry jam when I was little.

Even with medication, Toby's leg continued to give him

trouble. The arthritis occasionally made it difficult for him to walk comfortably, so he had to call in sick on a couple of Wednesdays. Because it was difficult for him to manage stairs during an arthritis flare-up—he fell down the staircase twice—Christopher carried him when he was in pain, cradling ninety pounds of dog like a newborn baby. "Morning, Toby! Do you want to go out?" Christopher would ask as he lifted him from his favorite spot in our bedroom, where he basked in the sunshine, stretching to welcome the day. Toby would do a lying-down rendition of the morning happy dance, making us laugh through our sadness.

Watching Christopher carry Toby up and down the stairs and out to the backyard on such days made my heart flutter. What an act of love! As I watched him nurture Toby more each day, I fell deeper in love with my husband. After so long together, I was pleasantly surprised that my affection for Chris could continue to grow. It made me wonder at the depth of feeling that might exist between us twenty, thirty, or forty years down the road.

Hmmm, I thought. Another lesson inspired by Toby.

Thirty-two

The Good Times

"Chris," I said, "were you really prepared to give Toby up that night after the incident with the knife block?"

Hearing his name, Toby lifted his head and gave me a warning look. I wasn't worried. Either he was too tired to run to the bathroom to bang the toilet seat up and down, or he'd become resigned to the fact that we would talk about him whether he locked himself in the bathroom or not.

"Yup," Chris said. "I was sure it was going to happen. I was positive there was no way you could talk me out of giving him up—even though you can be pretty persuasive."

He stared into his wine for a moment. "But you know, although I can remember being furious with Toby, completely steaming mad, it's hard for me to believe now that he could have ever made me feel that way. In fact, I haven't felt that way about anything in a long time."

I realized this was true. Chris didn't lose his temper anymore. Neither of us got too bothered about stuff going wrong. We had both learned to take things in stride, to accept difficulties, to forgive others. We had both learned to be more like Toby in terms of forgiving and moving on.

"Are you glad we kept him?" I asked.

"Are you kidding?" Christopher looked at me with astonishment. "I'm a better person because of Toby. Not just because I'm more patient. I'm more relaxed, more open to just letting things go instead of having to control them. I know you are, too. Yeah, it's been hard sometimes—but it's been worth it."

The patients at the hospital would have agreed with him. Although they were excited if they got a job at the hospital or out in the community, they always missed seeing Toby on Wednesdays. Some patients who had been discharged would return on Wednesdays if they could just to visit with Toby. Even when patients on the unit found out they were going home, they had come to find the experience bittersweet. On his last Wednesday in the hospital, Amil cried and petted Toby for a long time. When I encouraged him to let Toby do a round of visiting, Charlene stopped me.

"We'll see Toby next week. Poor Amil has to go home." That cracked everyone up.

Holding Toby's head between his big palms, Amil looked Toby in the eyes. Toby gazed right back.

"You're the best dog, Toby. Thanks for hanging out with us here. You make being in the hospital a lot easier."

Toby licked Amil's wrist.

"Toby makes me miss my own dog. If you ever don't want Toby anymore, Charmaine, he can live with me."

"Thanks, Amil. But I don't think there will ever be a day when I don't want Toby."

Sometimes it seemed like everyone wanted Toby. Invitations to events continued to pour in. Dogpalooza promised a day of Fido-friendly fun, an event at which a number of dog-related businesses have an outdoor expo. And a Fido friendly day it was. First, Chris and I walked Toby around the outdoor booths to get him used to the new surroundings. There were dog trainers, pet-assisted therapy programs, breeders, and stores that sold dog toys and other canine products. For Toby, this was like Disneyland. Dogs, treats, games, people, and balls! It took a while for him to settle down; Chris took him for several walks to burn off energy and help him get comfortable.

We were volunteering at the Chimo booth. Toby greeted people who stopped by, and Christopher and I handed out information and answered questions. The wind was blowing hard, and around us the tents covering the tables kept falling over. Hanging Toby's heavy knapsack from the frame of our tent as a weight to help hold it down, I was able to visit instead of holding the fabric in place. Many people looked at the *Chicken Soup for the Soul* book on display, stopping to ask about Toby. By now, I was a pro at telling Toby's story; I had told it at all his book signings and at our media and publicity events—and I never tired of it.

Jamie Hall, the pet writer for the *Edmonton Journal,* stopped by. We chatted and she added Toby's story to her pet blog—another outlet for our fame-loving hound. Meeting Jamie was a great opportunity, as she continued to blog about Toby and featured him, and his story, several more times in the paper.

Newspaper stories and special events weren't the only way people were learning about Toby. Christopher and I kept busy creating special bookmarks to promote Toby's website and Facebook page and to slip inside the books at signings. And I was busy writing weekly PAWsitive Inspirations about living life on purpose and with passion, as well as the many life lessons I am reminded of and taught through life with Toby. Because of Toby, we were far more engaged in our community than we had ever been, from participating in spring neighborhood and park clean ups with Toby to events like Dogpalooza.

The months flew by. With the holiday season approaching, there arose other opportunities for Toby to be in the limelight. "What about having him participate at the Christmas in the Heartlands event, Chris?" I asked. "We can share his story, inspire others to adopt a pet, and help out the NASAP rescue agency."

Upon arriving at the event, located in a small community hall in the country, Toby bounded into the building and greeted everyone in his usual exuberant fashion.

"Wow, Christopher, look at all these animals." I pointed to the puppies and dogs running everywhere and the tables of rabbits and guinea pigs. Toby began playing with the dogs, barking happily. A little boy came over and threw a ball for Toby, who obediently chased it, scooped it up in his jaws, and brought it back. He barked at the boy, telling him to throw the ball again, but the kid had become interested in something else. But Toby wouldn't stop barking even when a lady from one of the rescue agencies tossed him an orange squeaky toy.

"Well," Chris muttered, "I don't know what's more annoying. The barking or the squeaky toy."

"Barking has my vote." When Toby barked on and on like this, I tended to get exhausted and crabby. We'd done so much training and come so far in other areas, it frustrated me that we couldn't get Toby to stop barking on command. "I am not listening to this all day," I said. "Let's get out of here early."

On the way home, Toby slept like a baby. "Looks like he tired himself out," I said.

Looking in the rearview mirror, Chris nodded. "Thank goodness! I hope he naps the whole way home."

Looking out the window at the snowy scenery passing by, I found myself thinking that we lived a similar life to my friends who had children. Like them, we ran here and there to participate in events with our child, sought support from the professionals who could help us, and basically scheduled our entire existence around Toby.

Life was good! I enjoyed the joy Toby brought us, even if it was complicated joy. Best of all, we had reached a turning point. The good days with Toby far outweighed the bad ones. We rarely endured his destructive behaviors, especially since by now we had become smart about them. We put all the shoes in a bin in the closet to make closet-emptying days easier to clean up after. Bowl spinning, toilet seat flipping, and nudging shower doors remained a fairly regular part of Toby's routine, although they annoyed us less now.

In fact, these good days inspired me to develop a workshop with Toby. I called it Working on Purpose and structured it so that Toby would share the stage with me. I had no idea how it would work out for either of us. To test the workshop, I delivered it to the people at Chimo.

"The audience is made up of dog lovers, so at least they can help with Toby if he gets rambunctious," I told Christopher.

"But will the workshop have relevance to anyone other than dog owners?" he asked. Chris is always thinking strategically. But this time, I was one step ahead of him.

"Many of the lessons I've learned from Toby are very relevant to business. He's taught me about work/life harmony, bringing passion into the workplace, inspired performance, being focused, and keeping your eye on the goal. These are all lessons that will be of value to business people."

The workshop began with Toby's story. At the break, Chris mentioned that every time I said Toby's name, he looked over at me, awaiting direction. I would have to figure out how to give him something to do if I wanted to avoid causing him stress or have him act up.

Still, Toby did great. At one point, I glanced over and saw him, the star of the night, lying with one leg hanging casually over the front of the stage and his head on his paws, smiling at the audience. A lump welled in my throat and a tear slid down my cheek. *Look how far our Toby has come.*

Every year on Toby's anniversary of starting his volunteer work, the hospital sends Toby a PetSmart gift card and a thank-you card. Chimo also recognized Toby and the other pets through volunteer recognition days. The day we received Toby's Chimo Project award was another day of absolute pride—and, perhaps, a foreshadowing of great things in the future. Sadly, because we were out of town, we could not attend the volunteer appreciation event and receive the award in person, but it was mailed to our home.

Reading the certificate and letter, I smiled at the words that were addressed to Toby and me:

> Congratulations! You have been awarded the Reese Award by The Chimo Animal Assisted Therapy Project. This award is named after Reese, a Great Pyrenees who was a certified therapy animal of The Chimo Project and volunteered for two years before he passed away from bone cancer. Reese made an indelible mark on all who knew him and exemplified what it means to be a great therapy animal.
>
> Good job, Toby.

Yes, good job, Toby!

On Toby's Terms

As it turned out, we *did* have to give up on Toby—but in a different way from what Christopher had intended on that long-ago night. When we gave up trying to make him the perfect dog and built on his strengths instead, he was able to concentrate on his purpose and the things that brought him joy. Learning this lesson changed our lives forever.

In the lake the day of our sailboat accident, Christopher had had the strength to surrender to fate, to accept whatever the outcome would be. But we didn't learn the lesson then. Instead, our perfectionism and desire to control things kicked into high gear, and the benefits of taking action and charting our paths obscured the disadvantages of that desire for control. We couldn't just relax and enjoy the adventure that is life.

Through Toby, we learned the art of giving up in situations in which control is an illusion. Once we stopped trying to change our dog, Christopher and I were able to concentrate on our own purposes and the things that brought us joy. As we became more comfortable and accepting of our situation and of Toby, all three of us were happier and more productive.

As I write this, Toby is lying beside my office chair. Soon my ninety minutes will be up, and he will nudge at me to tell me it's time to play. If I don't respond, he'll bump my arm or leg again, and may even wheel me out of the office toward the things he considers top priority.

But I still have some time.

Toby continues to spin his food dish almost daily, closet emptying incidents still happen several times a month, bouts of wanton destruction still occur from time to time, and his barking continues to be a challenge. He still sits with his head on my desk, watching me work and nudging my arm, sometimes spilling my coffee.

But we love him more every day.

Time is moving quickly, but I'm making the most of it. So is Toby. He'll soon be nine years old. Regardless of the month or the weather, mornings are always our favorite time of day. Waking up at home or the cottage to sunshine and fresh air is a source of joy. Toby continues to greet Chris and me in the morning with his happy dance or a series of gentle nudges to our faces to announce that a new day has arrived. Toby begins each day with gratitude and forgiveness and a willingness to start anew. This has become my waking attitude as well.

It is true that, as pet owners, we often give to our pets. However, in the giving, we receive so much more—through animals, we see our own reflections. When our pets misbehave or act peculiarly, we have an opportunity to look at ourselves to see what is really going on . . . not with them but with us. Often, when Toby becomes anxious or fussy, he is responding to an emotion he sees or senses in me. To recognize this, however, we must be extremely present and open to this degree of self-reflection. Typically, Toby will be the one to tap me on the shoulder and say *Char, chill out, you're stressed!* before I even recognize this in myself—and I consider myself to be a very proactive, present, and self-aware person. It makes me wonder how many of us stroll through life on autopilot, missing precious moments.

Toby's fan club continues to grow, and he still often makes appearances at special events. The neighborhood children call him regularly for play dates. The ever-increasing circle of people who know and care about him continues to astound me. This dog was meant to do big things, to make his playground in life as big as possible, and bring joy to everyone who entered it. Watching him has led me to wish for a bigger playground, too, and with the help of my coach and through my own self-development work, I'm expanding mine and having more fun. I am completely living my passion and working with purpose.

Christopher and I even turned to Toby when rebranding our twelve-year-old business, which was once called Hammond Mediation & Consulting Group Inc. Now it is Hammond International Inc., and the brand is summed up by the following Toby-inspired statement: "Bounce Forward with

Charmaine Hammond—Building Resilient and Inspired Teams." It's just one of the adventures in our lives that have been inspired by our incorrigible but adorable dog.

There's no doubt that Toby has been expensive. We are probably the only couple on the planet that orders toilet tank lids in bulk, getting very strange looks from the store clerks. We've replaced more toilet flusher handles than ten families could use in a lifetime, because Toby delights in chewing them beyond recognition. Vet bills have added up. The costs continue to mount. When Toby recently attempted to remove the fence boards, possibly in a bid for freedom, Christopher was forced to replace the gate; and when Toby chewed the boards from the bottom up in an effort to escape during a storm, those had to be replaced too.

Other things we simply live with. The lid of our back-yard composter will never fit properly again, but has served as an apparently delicious chew toy. We have not yet enjoyed an apple off our two-year-old tree because Toby gets to them first, devouring them before they are ripe enough for our taste. We continue to open our front door with our hands over our ears, apologizing profusely for the noise to unsuspecting deliverymen and Girl Guides. We wonder what our front hall closet will look like when we arrive home. Toby's snoring routinely wakes us in the middle of the night. And on the days that Toby's arthritis is causing him pain, Chris still carries our dog up and down the stairs. And in those moments, I fall more in love with Chris.

Despite all this, one thing is clear. We would infinitely rather live on Toby's terms than live on our own terms without Toby.

Book Club Discussion Questions

1. What were the most poignant lessons that Toby taught his owners, Charmaine and Christopher? What is the most profound lesson you learned from your own pet?

2. Clearly this dog is a handful—and on occasion, the couple come close to surrendering him to the local shelter. But they stick it out and then fall in love with him. How did this couple grow, both individually and in their marriage, as a result of their life with Toby? In what way did this couple enhance Toby's emotional and physical health? How would you have dealt with a dog like Toby?

3. Charmaine discusses her tendency toward being a perfectionist and all-or-nothing thinking—a trait that is also shared to some degree by her husband, Chris. How did this trait affect their relationship and marriage? How did it impact their relationship with Toby? Do you think that you are a perfectionist? Why or why not?

4. The author and her husband survive a life-threatening experience. How did this incident impact them, and in what ways did it change their lives? In what way did bringing Toby into their lives allow them to relive the

lessons learned that day? Do you think you would have responded the same way or differently?

5. The couple are told by a behaviorist that Toby "lacks purpose" and clarity on his role in the family. In what ways did helping Toby discover his purpose modify his behavior? How would you define your "purpose" and in what way do you deem it necessary to living with passion?

6. "Letting go" is a theme throughout the story. What is the relevance of "letting go" and in what way does doing so change the author's life? Have you ever had to "let go" of something? How did that affect you?

7. In what way is Toby an inspiration? In this story, who inspired you the most and for what reason? Who or what inspires you?

8. Charmaine alludes to the axiom, "When the student is ready, the teacher appears." Who was the teacher—the author or Toby? Of the lessons each learned, what was the most significant? Are you a teacher, student, or both? Explain.

9. When Toby tips over the keepsake box, what hidden treasures surprise Charmaine? How do these discoveries impact Chris and Charmaine's future with Toby? Do you have a box of "hidden treasures"? What memories do they evoke?

10. What kept Christopher from all but giving up on Toby? How did this decision affect the couple's marriage and their plans for their future? Facing the same sort of situation, would you have given up or stuck with it? Why?

11. Charmaine comes off as an optimist, seeing the good in situations. How does this mindset both help and hinder her? Do you consider yourself optimistic or pes-

simistic? How does this view affect your life? Do you think you should change?

12. As Charmaine and Chris became the "pack leaders" in Toby's life, his behavior improved. Had they accepted this sooner, would the outcome have been different? What qualities do pack leaders emulate? When have you been a pack leader in your life? How did being a pack leader change a situation for you?

About the Author

CHARMAINE HAMMOND is a former correctional officer, mediator, and facilitator with more than twenty-five years experience facilitating individual and corporate development.

Charmaine is president of Hammond International Inc., an international consulting firm, and works nationwide building highly productive and motivated teams. She is member of the Canadian Association of Professional Speakers and speaks to audience around the world.

In 2009, her story "Volunteering from the Heart" was featured in *Chicken Soup for the Soul: What I Learned from the Dog.* Currently, Charmaine and Toby are on a book and speaking tour, conducting "dog-author" book signings throughout the US and Canada.

Charmaine lives in Alberta, Canada, with her husband, Christopher, and their precocious dog, Toby, who—when he is not rearranging their house—works as a volunteer pet-assisted therapy dog.

Her next book, *GPS Your Best Life,* co-authored with Debra Kasowski, is due out in 2011 (Bettie Youngs Books Publishers, www.BettieYoungsBooks.com).

You can contact Charmaine via her website at www.hammondgroup.biz, or follow her on Twitter and Facebook.

TOBY is a media magnet who has won several awards, including Chimo's prestigious Reese award, named in honor of a Great Pyrenees dog who died from bone cancer after an outstanding volunteer career. In addition to hundreds of media appearances, serving as guest of honor at grand openings, and being the sponsor of the Sherwood Park Phoenix Girls Elite Soccer Team, Toby will star as himself in a film about his fascinating life. A media sensation, Toby has his own blog and website. Visit Toby at www.OnTobysTerms.com, www.tobytales.com, or follow him on Facebook.

Other Books by Bettie Youngs Books

The Maybelline Story . . . and the Spirited Family Dynasty Behind It

Sharrie Williams

A woman's most powerful possession is a man's imagination.
—Maybelline ad, 1934

In 1915, when a kitchen-stove fire singed his sister Mabel's lashes and brows, Tom Lyle Williams watched in fascination as she performed what she called "a secret of the harem"—mixing petroleum jelly with coal dust and ash from a burnt cork and applying it to her lashes and brows. Mabel's simple beauty trick ignited Tom Lyle's imagination, and he started what would become a billion-dollar business, one that remains a viable American icon after nearly a century. He named it Maybelline in her honor.

Throughout the twentieth century, the Maybelline company inflated, collapsed, endured, and thrived in tandem with the nation's upheavals. Williams—to avoid unwanted scrutiny of his private life—cloistered himself behind the gates of his Rudolph Valentino Villa and ran his empire from a distance. Now, after nearly a century of silence, this true story celebrates the life of an American entrepreneur, a man forced to remain behind a mask, using his sister-in-law Evelyn Boecher—a charismatic, hard-boiled, commandingly beautiful woman—as his eyes to the world. A fascinating tale of ambition, luck, greed, secrecy, and, above all, love and forgiveness. A tale both epic and intimate, alive with the clash, the hustle, the music, and dance of American enterprise.

A richly told juicy story of a forty-year, white-hot love triangle that fans the flames of a major worldwide conglomerate.

—Neil Shulman, associate producer, *Doc Hollywood*

An insider's view into the genesis and building of a corporate giant. A wild ride of drama, and greatness.

—Alan Ragland, son of Maybelline legend "Rags Ragland"

ISBN 978-0-9843081-1-8 • $16.95

Out of the Transylvania Night

Aura Imbarus

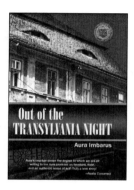

An epic tale of identity, love, and the indomitable human spirit.

Communist dictator Nicolae Ceausescu had turned Romania into a land of zombies as surely as if Count Dracula had sucked its lifeblood. Yet Aura Imbarus dares to be herself: a rebel among the gray-clad, fearful masses. Christmas shopping in 1989, Aura draw sniper fire as Romania descends into the violence of a revolution that topples one of the most draconian regimes in the Soviet bloc. With a bit of Hungarian mysticism in her blood, astonishingly accurate visions lead Aura into danger—as well as to the love of her life. They marry and flee a homeland still in chaos. With only two pieces of luggage and a powerful dream, they settle in Los Angeles where freedom and sudden wealth challenge their love as powerfully as Communist tyranny.

Aura loses her psychic vision, heirloom jewels are stolen, a fortune is lost, followed by divorce. But their early years as lovers in a war-torn country and their rich family heritage is the glue that reunites them. They pay a high price for their materialistic dreams, but gain insight and a love that is far richer. *Out of the Transylvania Night* is a deftly woven narrative about finding greater meaning and fulfillment in both free and closed societies. An incredibly powerful memoir: a story of tyranny, freedom, love, and identity.

Aura's courage shows the degree to which we are all willing to live lives centered on freedom, hope, and an authentic sense of self. Truly a love story!

—Nadia Comaneci, Olympic gold medalist

If you grew up hearing names like Tito, Mao, and Ceausescu but really didn't understand their significance, read this book!

—Mark Skidmore, Paramount Pictures

This book is sure to find its place in memorial literature of the world.

—Beatrice Ungar, editor-in-chief, *Hermannstädter Zeitung*

ISBN 978-0-9843081-2-5 • $14.95

Diary of a Beverly Hills Matchmaker

by Marla Martenson

The inside scoop from the Cupid of Beverly Hills, who has brought together countless couples who have gone on to live happily ever after. But for every success story there are ridiculously funny dating disasters with high-maintenance, out-of-touch, impossible to please, dim-witted clients!

Marla takes her readers for a hilarious romp through her days as an LA matchmaker and her daily struggles to keep her self-esteem from imploding in a town where looks are everything and money talks. From juggling the demands her out-of-touch clients, to trying her best to meet the capricious demands of an insensitive boss, to the ups and downs of her own marriage to a Latin husband who doesn't think that she is "domestic" enough, Marla writes with charm and self-effacement about the universal struggles all women face in their lives. Readers will laugh, cringe, and cry as they journey with her through outrageous stories about the indignities of dating in Los Angeles, dealing with overblown egos, vicariously hobnobbing with celebrities, and navigating the wannabe-land of Beverly Hills. In a city where perfection is almost a prerequisite, even Marla can't help but run for the Botox every once in a while.

Marla's quick wit will have you rolling on the floor.

—**Megan Castran, international YouTube Queen**

Sharper than a Louboutin stiletto, Martenson's book delivers!

—**Nadine Haobsh,** *Beauty Confidential*

ISBN 978-0-9843081-0-1 • $14.95

BETTIE YOUNGS BOOKS

.

. . . books that inspire
and celebrate
remarkable journeys

VISIT OUR WEBSITE AT
www.BettieYoungsBooks.com